# My Battle & Beyond

### Silent Journey
### Living with Sarcoidosis

D.F. Ireland

By the same Author

Cookbook
Grandmama's Treasured Favorites & Traditional Recipes

Disclaimer:

Information gathered to prepare this book originated from the author's personal diary, medical records, public materials from *Krames Patient Education, and Uptodate. The names of the* professionals described in this book are not authentic.

ISBN-13: 978-1506119694
ISBN-10:1506119697

Copyright 2015- Dianne Ireland
Cover Design – Dianne Ireland
Printed by - Create Space

*"I have
chosen to be
HAPPY
because it is
good for
my health"*

-Voltaire

*"There is only one way
to happiness
and
that is to cease worrying
about things
which are beyond
the power of our will"*

-Epictetus

## DEDICATION

To all my Sarc sisters, and brothers wherever you are, to believe in yourselves, and those around you.

Some days you will be the light for others, and some days you will need some light from them. As long as there is light, there is hope, and there is a way.

Sarcoidosis sufferers are known as snowflakes. No two snowflakes are alike; no two people suffering with Sarcoidosis are alike.

Stay strong with hopes there will be a cure for Sarcoidosis.

Please don't let another snowflake melt away!

BELIEVE; HOPE; LOVE; FAITH

# CONTENTS

# ACKNOWLEDGEMENT

I would like to acknowledge my precious family, who are continually there for me, especially my hubby Jim, who patiently waits in the many waiting rooms for me, while I have been in surgeries and numerous tests. Thank you, to my family, my rocks!

Huge thanks, to my wonderful medical team of professionals who saved my life; and to the western medical professionals, and holistic traditional professionals who work diligently to ensure my medical care and treatment plan is continually monitored, and effective.

And to my friends, and co-workers who offer continued encouragement with their kind words of caring.

I wish to acknowledge four women; who have been part of the finalization of my book.

Judy Coates; who has inspired me to write, her kind, and gentle way of reviewing my manuscript.

Tracy Zweifel; offering to review my manuscript, as she spoke of being honored. It is I, who is honored to have a wise women taking the time from her busy schedule to review my manuscript.

Dianne Tchir; thanks for editing my book, and encouraging me to continue to write, as she stated, "There is so much more in you."

Bernadette Harris; who endured the freezing snowy winter day, spending time with me, taking photo shots for the cover of my book, a vision I had.

Although neither one of us are professional photographers, and with several attempts, successfully produced a picture for my book; even when the camera froze up.

Sincere thank you ladies, for making this book become a reality.

And to the reader, thank you for taking this journey with me.

# PROLOGUE

"My life, My story, My silent journey"

As I turned the pages of my personal medical reports, I began to ponder over my circumstances, realizing the importance to share with others; my silent inner struggles, experiences, feelings about living, managing, and coping with a mysterious complicated disease, and the anguish it causes. As this may assist others who are suffering and letting them know they are not alone.

It was early spring in 2009, when my journey began to unravel with many ups, and downs battling the unknown; a roller coaster ride not knowing when the ride would stop. Experiencing various levels of emotions, and turmoil's at the same time. I was determine never to lose this fight, and to overcome.

I am living with Sarcoidosis, an autoimmune system disease, which effects, and damages one or more organs of the body. This is a mysterious disease, treated with prednisone, and chemotherapies.

It tends to be more common in women than men, between the ages of twenty to forty years of age. However, it can affect all ages and races. Sarcoidosis is most commonly found in African-American's and Northern European's. But in North America, African-Americans are attacked more frequently, and most severely than Caucasian, and are treated with prednisone, and chemotherapies. Sarcoidosis is characterized by a persistent nodular inflammation of the tissues. Lungs, lymph nodes, eyes, skin, liver and spleen which are most often involved, but almost any tissue or organ of the body can be affected.

Each individual, who has been diagnosed with Sarcoidosis, receives the same or similar treatments at various levels. This depends upon the severity of the disease, and organ location.

There are people who may unknowingly have had Sarcoidosis, and the disease stabilized on its own. There are others who have Sarcoidosis in only one area; particularly the lungs which is most common.

Then, there are individuals like myself, where the disease has affected a number of my organs, causing severe problems. I have Sarcoidosis in the trachea, heart, lymph nodes (throughout my body), eyes, outer skin of my left leg, outer upper left eyelid and bridge of my nose, and have been identified as, at a higher risk level.

In the preparation of this book, was not my aim to present happenings from a professional standpoint of views, as I am not a medical professional. Only to share my personal story of diagnosis, treatments, options, and prognosis which I have had, and continue to endure.

My search for resources, and potential alternative treatments kept me strong in hope, and faith as I continue to struggle with nagging pain.

I encourage those who are currently affected by, and those who have recently been diagnosed with Sarcoidosis to continue your personal research on ways to aid with your discomforts and pain. "Stay strong, believe in yourself!"

For me it is important to keep my spirit strong.

My hope is that the reader will have a better understanding of Sarcoidosis disease effects, and the many challenges individuals may encounter when diagnosed with Sarcoidosis.

I sincerely hope that those of you who are currently affected by, and those who have currently been diagnosed with Sarcoidosis, take the journey to arrive at some comforts.

And, with blessings from the Creator, I pray for a healing of this disease.

So, come walk with me, as I tell my story.

Hiy Hiy Blessings

# ONE
## Visit to the Doctor

My journey begins on a relatively warm, sunny, winter day of January 8, 2009 as I recall, no different than any other day.

At sixty years of age, my health was normal; no high blood pressure, no illness, and rarely sick with any type of flus or colds. I was medication free with few doctor appointments.

I had scheduled a doctor's appointment, for that afternoon as I had concerns, and questions related to post-menopause. During the examination, Doctor Karen asked, "Do you have any other questions, relating to health issues?" "Yes I do. When I use my exercise machine, and move my arms back, and forth there is a crunching feeling, and heaviness in the center of my breast bone." As I pointed to the area.

Doctor Karen quickly checked the area; asking a few more questions, "I am going to order a chest x-ray, to be done this afternoon," she added. I never thought too much about it, I left the doctor's office, and drove across town to the Peace River Community Health Centre, for the x-ray. After the x-ray was completed, I went home, and carried on with my normal routine, waiting for the doctor's telephone call for the results, which I received a couple of days later.

And this is when my life changed, embarking on an unknown journey.

# TWO
## Findings

My x-ray results identified markings of lesions located along the trachea, the main airway by which air enters the lungs. Unsure of what these lesions could be Doctor Karen ordered a series of blood tests, which didn't provide any answers or didn't indicate anything abnormal. My question was, "Could the blood tests show if cancer was present?" This was the only thing I could think of, and I knew   she could not make any assumptions until knowing exactly what these lesions were, so more tests were ordered. But to no avail, there was nothing unusual. Doctor Karen made connections with other Doctors and Specialists.

I kept thinking, "What could it be? What do I tell my family or how, especially when nothing was confirmed." Tears swelled, about to flow, but I'd hold them back. No one can see me like this. This is so frustrating. Never in my life, had I ever been put into a situation of not knowing or understanding what my medical problems were. My whole life seemed to be in fast forward motion, like a spinning top, whirling, and whirling not knowing when or where it was going to stop. I had future plans, places to go, things to do, and I didn't need to be in this chaotic state.

I continued to have heaviness in my chest, even after I stopped exercising. I had many sleepless nights, and a difficult time staying focused at work. Waiting for further news was unbearable. I was on an emotional roller coaster filled with fear of the unknown.

# THREE
## Angel Has Arrived

However, when facing difficult circumstances, I often reflected on my past, where I came from, and who I was. The times spent with my loved ones, brought me back to an afternoon, sitting around my parent's kitchen table having a cup of tea. A conversation led to my childhood, especially my birth, including detailed happenings of my lengthy arrival, along with the painful, and emotional experience my parents endured, with the birth of their first baby.

Dad told me the story of my arrival: a difficult delivery which took a week and how Doctor Sutherland had to use forceps (a hand-held instrument for grasping, holding or pulling objects) to pull me out of the birth canal. I guess I gave the Doctor quite a fight.

I emerged on a winter November day, screaming, and gulping in every breath of air. However, as Mom described, I looked like I had just come through a battle of sorts, with scrapes, and some bruising on my shoulders, face and head. When she first held me, parts of my little body were wrapped with cloth bandages. Mom was afraid that I might be scarred for life. Mom said, "We were fortunate to have a healthy baby. Some of the women, who had delivered babies during this time period, did not survive. During that November there were ten infants born, and only four survived." I remember my mom saying, "And you were one of those babies."

Now, I call that stubbornness or strong willed.

As our conversation continued, Mom explained, "In the old Peace River Municipal Hospital, (where she went as it was close to our farm where we lived) there were only one, four bed maternity ward. In that era, the hospitals were built without private maternity wards. Babies were placed in a nursery, and brought to their mothers at feeding time. It was sad remembering, how upset it was for a woman in the next bed. Her baby was one that did not survive. I'll never forget that time." Dad proudly made the comment, "I was their angel."

I cannot thank my parents enough, for telling their story, even though it took nearly fifty plus years to share their experiences, of my arrival into this beautiful world. I had never heard my Dad talk so much, and how he expressed the importance of having a healthy bouncing baby girl.

Angel had arrived!

My parents were informed by Doctor Sutherland, that I would be their only child, as he felt my mother would not be able to conceive more children. Within two and half years, to the Doctor's surprise, my mother gave birth to a set of twin girls, then fourteen months later a son and several years later a girl.

'Mom and Dad were blessed with not only one angel, but five little angels.'

# FOUR
# Roller Coaster Ride

As time went by, Doctors and Medical Specialists were reviewing my charts, x-rays and discussing a medical plan of action.

Shortly after the first x-ray, Doctor Karen scheduled an appointment for me with Doctor Beak, Specialist in Grande Prairie, about a two hour drive from home.

At that time my blood tests were normal, my lymph nodes were not swollen, and I had no pain, just this weird feeling in my chest, and those markings on my trachea. If my lymph nodes had been swollen, (lymphadenopathy, an abnormal enlargement of the lymph node) a biopsy procedure would have taken place by draining fluid off for testing.

Doctor Beak explained, "There is a possibility of lymphoma cancer," and he wanted to do further testing, an exploratory surgery, since there was no other way to discover what these lesions were. Hearing this, my internal body went absolutely numb. The word cancer and the seriousness in the tone of his voice made my heart beat rapidly, and at that point, my emotions became uncontrollable. I felt my eyes fill with tears. But I was determined not to cry, to be brave, and face what came next. At that moment I felt completely alone, even though Doctor Beak was sitting in front of me, and my husband sitting in the chair next to me. The word cancer was swimming around in my head, like waves splashing the shoreline.

Doctor Beak quickly assessed my situation and tried to assure me, that I would have many years ahead of me to enjoy life, and all my plans. I felt this was a death sentence; my life was spinning like a top, going faster, and faster.

As our conversation continued, Doctor Beak immediately took charge. He informed me that he was going to start making arrangements to have me scheduled for surgery that day or that evening. Then he explained the seriousness of the operation, especially the location, as the lesions were along the trachea next to a main artery. This surgery would determine what these lesions were.

I had no idea a visit to a Specialist would lead to surgery the very same day. I was not prepared, this was supposed to be a day trip, and my intensions were to go to my appointment, and then, go shopping. Now my plans drastically changed.

Before I left the doctor's office, he informed my husband and me that arrangements were already being made, as we spoke, and I would be contacted by phone sometime in the next few hours. To ease the pressures of what my husband and I had just heard, we decided to carry on as planned, do our shopping, and wait in the city for the call. This would also keep us occupied, and not focused on the conversation that had just taken place in the doctor's office. Unknown to me, many phone calls were being made back and forth, with Doctor Karen at home, and to other Specialists, determining when and who would be performing the surgery.

By midafternoon, I had not heard anything, so we decided to drive home. We were almost on the outskirts of the city, when my phone rang, and on the other end was the voice of Doctor Beak. He informed me, plans had been changed and the surgery would not take place today, and I should expect a call from another Specialist from Edmonton, a five hour drive south. This information made me even more nervous, yet relieved at the same time. I can't explain how I really felt, maybe confused, numb and motionless all at once. But I was breathing a bit of relief.

Our drive home was mostly in silence. Possibly we were both thinking worst case scenarios, and still with no confirmed results. We had so many questions.

## FIVE
# Blessed

It was difficult telling my children, and to let them know what was happening, and that there was an unconfirmed possibility of me having cancer. They listened in silence, then smiled, and said that they understood and everything would be okay. Oh, how I love my family.

For many days, and at any time of the day, I prayed to my Creator, asking him to watch over me, and help me get through this mystery. I did not know what I had. I only knew I was going for exploratory surgery. As I have always been an optimistic person, staying positive, and carried on with some normality.

I informed my supervisors at my work places, (as I had two split positions), letting them know that I was waiting for a call for surgery. Finally, the day came, I received my call. I was scheduled for exploratory surgery, and of all days on April 1$^{ST}$. I'm thinking, "April Fool's Day, I cannot believe my surgery would be that day?"  For some reason it didn't seem fair. Now, it was time to tell my supervisors, which I managed without becoming too emotional.

Coincidentally, I was off work for ten days at the school as it was Easter Holidays. None of the staff, except the supervisor, and one other staff member knew my situation. Some of the staff were planning to travel to warmer climates on their break. At the school I worked as a Career Coordinator, and my other half-time position, at the hospital, as Manager of a Prenatal and Nutrition Program. I was also fortunate to be able to flex my days at the hospital.

The one thing I dreaded the most was telling my mom. I really didn't have detailed information for her, so I decided not to say anything. The day before my scheduled exploratory surgery, my husband and I left home to travel to Edmonton. Somehow, someone leaked the information to my mom that I was going to the city for surgery. We were halfway to the city when she called me on my phone, asking "What is going on?" I had to tell her that I was going for exploratory surgery, and not to worry. This was one of my hardest days talking to my mom on a cellular phone, and hoping she would not be too upset. Life was not fair and it was very hard to inform my elderly parent, who lives alone,(as my dad had passed on a few years prior) that her first born was going for surgery, but could not explain what for, only exploratory.

We arrived in the city, settled into our hotel room on Kingsway Street, and waited for the next day. I had a phone conversation with my daughter, and then I called my friend, both who lived in the city, and both who gave me reassurance. It seemed that my supports were all in place. Unknown to me, my daughter had made arrangements with her supervisor to have the day off, and my friend informed me that she would be at the hospital, when I woke up. It was great to have a cheering team; so much love and encouragement from my husband, daughter and friend. Throughout that evening and into the long difficult night many thoughts came and went. I was thankful for my support team here in the city and back home.

Once again, I had to be a trooper, not to tear up and get all emotional. I have always been a fairly strong individual, and I felt that no matter the outcome, I would find a way to cope.

# SIX
# Exploratory Surgery

April 1, 2009, I arrived early in the morning, at the Royal Alexandra Hospital. I walked down a corridor to the specified area, to register about one hour prior to my surgery. After I was prepared for Bronchoscopy Mediastinoscopy surgery, blood typed and an intravenous inserted, I waited in a small cubical. At this time, lying in my bed I felt over-come with loneliness. Fear of the unknown, and having no control of the situation crept into my space. So many theories were going through my mind. "What could it be? What would the findings be?" A lot of what if's, floated through my head, and I wondered what kind of future lay ahead of me. My subconscious whirled, as I waited, which felt like forever. I was supposed to enjoy life to the fullest, spend time with my children, grandchildren, and family members. Hug my grandchildren, listen to their everyday happenings and go to their activities. I was to enjoy future retirement, which was not that far away, and travel to far-away places.

When my turn finally came, I was wheeled in my bed into a dimly lit surgical waiting area. I looked around the room thinking, "This location feels like an assembly line, beds are side by side in cubicles. Everyone waited their turn to enter through the doors of an operating room." While lying there waiting my turn, I reflected on what took place days before, and the discussion with the Doctor and my family members. I had so many questions which kept slipping in and out of my mind, almost like I was dreaming. "Was I dreaming?"

At one point tears slide down my cheeks, I silently scolded myself, "No tears, dam it, be tough." I was going to get through this ordeal, as I felt I needed to stay strong for my family. I guess it's the mama bear in me. And have you ever tried to tell yourself to be tough, when you're lying in a narrow bed with only a gaudy green night shirt on?

When my turn came, my bed was rolled into the operating room. I was moved from the bed onto an even narrower slab covered with a white sheet. I thought to myself, "It was a good thing I was no three hundred pounder, because I was sure to fall off." Next it was time for anesthesia, a quick way to go to sleep, "Okay this is not where I want to be, oh dam, and I am not very good at being put to sleep, even with my permission." The Anesthetist placed the face mask over my mouth and nose, and it was lights out. I was in dream land.

Time must have flown by, because I was soon back in my cubical to recover. As I slowly opened my eyes, everything seemed foggy, and then as the haze cleared, the first person I saw was my husband, with a calm but serious face, sitting beside my bed. Then I heard other voices, my daughter, and then my friend. The first thing that came to my mind was, "Hurray, I made it, I am back to my world." I felt light headed and noticed there were a number of gadgets and wires attached to me. And I could feel a taped square shaped non-flexible white gauze on my neck, just under my chin, which limited my movement.

Since this was an early morning surgery, a day surgery, and once I recovered, I was released. I was out the door, on my way back to the hotel room by mid-afternoon. Pills were prescribed for pain, if needed and a list of soft foods, which I was supposed to eat for the next few hours but no milk products.

My daughter offered to go to the store next to our hotel, to shop. She found purchasing something that was already cooked without milk was difficult to find. I don't think anyone really pays any attention, how food is prepared, and what are the detailed ingredients, until one needs to go and purchase particular items. After my daughter came back from the store, we decided to go for dinner in the hotel dining room. I hadn't eaten all day, and I was famished.

Before going for dinner, I was having pain along with discomfort, so I decided to take one of the prescribed pills. Not a good idea, which I found out shortly after, after taking only one forkful of food. I became nauseous to my stomach, and felt like I was about to vomit. I quickly went to my room to rest, leaving everyone at the dinner table.

My five hundred kilometer ride home was comfortable enough, except I looked like a goose, stretching its neck for its next feed. The big white bandage stuck on my neck restricted any movement of my neck.

In a prior conversation with Doctor Azim, Surgeon informed me that they were going to test the lesions for Tuberculosis, Lymphoma Cancer, Sarcoidosis and Fungus Infection.

For the next few days, I rested.

Doctor Karen called to inform me that she had received my report from the Surgical Pathology and the findings of my exploratory surgery indicated I had six lesions varying in sizes from seven milometers to thirty-seven milometers located along the trachea. Two of these lesions were found to be hard and discolored, and were removed for testing. The results confirmed Sarcoidosis.

Once I received this information, that I had Sarcoidosis, I did not know how to react. Although, I was relieved it was not cancer, but felt distressed and concerned about having Sarcoidosis. At this time I had no knowledge regarding this disease, and very little information was being shared. I only knew that it was a strange form of an unknown autoimmune disease.

Anyone I talked to had never heard of it, and I had no idea that this disease could damage other organs, affecting one's life severely. In my mind I had to accept my condition, and continue with life as is, so I decided to keep active with my daily routine, work, community involvement and spending time with my family.

Ten days went by, it was time to take off the bandage, and check how the incision healed. I was alone in the house, looking in the bathroom mirror at my reflection, and that white bandage. I began to prepare to remove the bandage, not sure what I would find, thinking the cut would be small, and slightly pink. As I took the bandage off slowly, my facial expressions in the reflection of the mirror changed. Shocked! Not at all what I expected! I became unsteady and squeezes to my stomach. I felt a wave of emotions wash over me looking at this ugly incision. I was horrified. What I saw was definitely not what I expected. What was I looking at? The incision was red, with black stitches, and blue black bruising all around the incision, along my neck and down across my chest. Now I felt faint and unsteady; however, I kept myself in check. Once again, I thought to myself, "Be brave, I can handle this, no matter what the outcome."

Although I was told that during surgery, the Surgeon lifted my breastbone to check for lesions on the heart and area, but I did not expect to see so much bruising. Later, remembering this conversation, I realized why my neck and chest areas were discolored although this gave me little comfort.

The holiday break was over, which meant it was time to go back to work. I am a private person, so, I camouflaged the discolored incision on my neck area with scarves. It may have looked like a fashionable style to others, but for me it was the questions that I was not prepared to answer. I found it was a delicate emotional subject, and this was my way of avoiding questions I didn't want to answer, particularly at this time.

As the weeks went by, my incision healed to a light pink color. I started to apply Vitamin E cream (to help healing and fading of the scar) daily to the area, hoping this cream would prevent the incision from marking my skin, leaving only a faint scar. Within a year the scar was slightly noticeable and smooth.

↔

In my family DNA health history, I could have had any of the suspected diseases as my grandfather on my dad's side had Tuberculosis, a communicable bacteria disease typically marked by wasting, fever and formation of cheesy tubercles often in the lungs.

Every year the immediate families were required to have a chest x-ray. Unfortunately my grandfather passed away from Tuberculosis.

↔

Then there are family members who have had cancer, with positive results; however, no sign of lymphoma: a cancer of the lymphatic system, the network of lymph vessels and the spleen, lymph nodes, and other tissues that filter the fluid (plasma) portion of the blood. – A tumor of lymphoid tissue.

↔

On my mother's side, there is a history of Graves, Wegener's Granulomatosis, Lupus and Leukemia disease.

↔

In reference to countries where Sarcoidosis disease is found, and with the findings of my family genealogy, country locations may have a connection, but this is not confirmed.

↔

My father's parents came from Hungary, and on my mother's side, her father came from England and her mother, my grandmother came from a long family history from the New York area of United States since the 1700's. With further research into my grandmother's genealogy, it is apparent that I am also a decent of African-American, Native Indian, German and Irish blood lines.

COULD ANY OF THESE BLOOD LINES BE IDENTIFIED AS SARCOIDOSIS CANDIDATES?

# SEVEN
# Life's Journey to Heal

Over the next year, I continued to have a series of tests, regular blood work, medical trips (sometimes more than once a month) to Edmonton. A five hundred kilometer road trip became a familiar path, knowing every curve, bump and of course my favorite coffee shops.

↔

My first testings' were completely unfamiliar to me, particularly the types of treatments and medical technologies used. I never required any extensive medical services before.

The first part of testing began with a CT scan of my lungs. I was not expecting what was to come next, as I lay on a narrow bed, and I mean narrow, with a large metal machine hanging from the ceiling and positioned at the far end of the bed. My instructions were, once a plastic hose was inserted into my mouth, I was to breathe normal as a liquid mist would be flowing through the tube. However, if I needed to take a break, I was to signal with my hand, as I was warned not to pull the hose out of my mouth unexpectedly, as a liquid mist of radiation may spray onto my face. As the procedure began, I placed the hose in my mouth, breathing at a normal rate, in and out with each breath. I was taking in a form of radiation mist at every two minute intervals, and then the procedure would stop a short period, and start again.

Try to imagine how long two minutes can be, as we rarely think about our breathing, and its regularity being timed by a clock. "I could almost hear a clock ticking, tick-tock." This became more difficult, as I became aware of my many senses, particularly my breathing and breathing sounds. I concentrated on my breathing, as if I were counting pushups.

As I continued to breathe in and out, a warm sensation flowed through my lungs. It felt as if a warm heating pad was placed onto my chest. Minutes after this procedure was completed, still lying motionless, the nurse informed me that an x-ray machine would now begin taking pictures. I watched as a large flat bottomed machine moved silently  above me, passing over the length of my  body, then  two side flat arms of white metal square blocks, moved close to my right and left sides. These metal arms were so close, as if they were going to give me a hug. I remember thinking at the time, "If this machine dropped, I would be squished as flat as a pancake." As the machine continued to move back and forth, under and over my body, recording data silently, the only sound I could hear was a low hum and the clicking of the keyboard, where the nurse sat viewing images on a monitor screen. This procedure was painless, except for a warm feeling in my lungs, which stayed with me for several hours.

That night, as I slid between the sheets of my bed, I chuckled then whispered to my husband, "I might be glowing in the dark." I could easily imagine my body shining brightly, with yellow sunrays, dancing all around the bed.

Several months passed. I had recovered from my exploratory surgery, and my incision healed, but my health did not improve. My energy level was extremely low, and I often felt short of breath. I was unable to walk any distance and this was not the norm. My husband and I routinely walked one kilometer every evening, walking through our neighborhood, taking advantage of the warm sunny summer weather, and enjoying short visits with neighbors.

During one of these evening walks, I walked about four blocks from our house and couldn't go any further, as my legs felt heavy and my chest hurt with an odd fluttery sensation with shortness of breath. My son, who happened to be coming over to visit, drove me back to our house.

I continued to feel tired all the time, and had absolutely no energy. As time went by, I couldn't climb stairs easily. My legs felt heavy, as if I was dragging a large metal ball through mud. Then there were other days when I had lots of energy, and there seemed to be nothing wrong. This carried on for the next few months, and I never thought too much about it, as I didn't realize, possibly it could be Sarcoidosis.

At this point, I had not researched further into the disease, and its affects. I didn't know Sarcoidosis could have major effects on my organs.

On one particular occasion, I had gone to the city for a meeting, planning to spend a bit of mother daughter quality time, shopping, visiting, having a good meal, and of course a movie. However, my daughter had to work part of the weekend, so I decided to take this opportunity to visit a long-time friend, and stay at her condo overnight. We had an enjoyable evening; first dinner followed by a glass of wine. My friend liked to talk, which was probably a good thing this time. I was sitting in the living room on a comfortable leather couch, glass of wine in my hand, relaxed, enjoying our conversation when, for whatever reason, something weird came over me. I seemed to drift out of my body, as if I was floating into darkness. It is difficult to describe what took place, as if I was in some sort of trance. I was physically sitting upright on the couch, looking straight at my friend, eyes open, but I couldn't see her. I was in total darkness, my vision had vanished, and I was blind looking into darkened space. I had feelings of passing out. My head was reeling and foggy, and fear crept into my body. In the distance, all I could hear was my friend talking, her voice drifting in and out. I focused on her voice, determined that I wouldn't fade away. This feeling passed within seconds, although it felt like an eternity. My vision cleared to normal, and my friend was still talking, unaware of what had just happened. My body felt a strange unsettled sensation, like it was someone else's, so I decided to sit very still, motionless, not moving a muscle, as I was afraid it may re-occur. I would just answer my talking friend when needed. After a time, not sure how much time I was back to feeling slightly normal. At first I thought it was the wine, although I only had one sip. I had never experienced anything like this before, and would not want to encounter this again.

I never mentioned my experience to anyone, and I am not sure if anyone would have understood. Or maybe I feared the worst, and did not want to admit I was really not well, and that something dangerous was happening to me.

Thankfully, the Creator was watching over me, and over the next many months, I often found myself praying.

As the year past, since my exploratory surgery, I continued to feel less than hundred percent. My health seemed to be deteriorating. I strived not to let any discomforts seize control of my body and mind, staying active, mentally focused on my goals, and believing each day to be a good day.

# EIGHT

# To Late

It was June 2010, school was almost completed for another year, and it was my grandchildren's school achievement, and award day. At lunch hour, I drove over to their school, and due to the number of parents attending the school function, the parking area was full. This meant I would have to park, and walk a few blocks to the school. Although I felt crappy, I sat and watched the hour and half ceremonies, feeling proud of my grandchildren's achievements. After the ceremonies I walked back to where I had parked my car, and by this time, my legs felt like heavy wooden posts unable to move with any ease. It became obvious that I should seek medical attention; so, I drove to the hospital where I worked in the afternoons.

Today I decided to park in the front public parking area, which is only for public use, instead of the one designated for staff. I walked across the parking lot, with great difficulty, as my legs still felt heavy, as if I was walking through thick mud, making every step unbearable. When I approached the Emergency Department, I informed the nurse, at the desk, that I would like my blood pressure checked because I was not feeling well. For some reason I thought my problem may be my blood pressure and not Sarcoidosis. After a few questions, I was directed to a small cubical where I was asked more questions, and then my blood pressure was checked. While taking my blood pressure, the nurse watched the monitor closely, and then in a quiet professional voice, said to me, as she removed the blood pressure arm cuff, "Come with me." I followed her to the critical room, nothing further was said, and except that I was directed to lie on the bed. At this point I was unaware of my situation, except there seemed to be a lot of commotion occurring around me. There were nurses coming and going, setting up the blood pressure machine, connecting electrocardiogram electrodes to my body, and an intravenous inserted into my right arm. Blood was drawn and then I was connected to an oxygen machine and a nose piece positioned in my nostrils. The nurses who worked around me seemed concerned, so I asked non-chalantly, "Should I be calling someone? No one knows that, I am at the Emergency Department. I am supposed to be in my office."

With concerned faces, I was told, "Yes, and tell them to pack you an overnight bag." I looked at them, and said, "What!" "Yes, you are not going anywhere."

Doctor Karen came in; (who happened to be on call) checked the monitors, left the room, and ordered electrocardiogram pads to be placed on me. "What for?" I asked. I was then told this was a precaution in case I went into cardiac arrest, and needed to use the paddles to resuscitate me. This not only surprised me, but made me unsure, and uncomfortable of all the happenings around me. All this time I wasn't sure what was going to happen to me medically, as I had no pain. With all this activity around me, and being hooked up to all sorts of wires, and monitors I felt concerned, but oblivious to my situation. I didn't realize the urgency, and importance to prevent a possible heart attack, as I did not realize at the time what my heart beat was.

I called my husband's cellular phone, explained to him where I was, what was happening, and to pack an overnight bag for me. He informed me that he wasn't close to home; he was on the work site a few miles out of town, but would come right away. Now, have you ever tried to explain what personal items to pack especially on a phone to your husband? This was quite a task in itself. I ended up describing what pieces of clothing to pack, along with personal items.

Then I phoned my son, to let him know what was happening. It seemed strange because I was at the school ceremonies with him and his wife, only an hour ago. Within only minutes, they walked into the room, my daughter-in-law took one look at the monitors, and without saying a word, turned, and walked out. She was the nurse in our family, and she quickly read these monitors, and knew exactly what was happening. She was on a mission to find out more information.

Shortly after, Doctor Karen returned, and announced, "You are going for a pacemaker." No general conversation on my condition, just stating going for a pacemaker. Now alarming bells were ringing in my head. Pacemaker?

My presumptions were that a pacemaker was for the elderly, as I had never inquired into why or how a pacemaker operates. Little did I know that many people of all ages have pacemakers for various heart related issues?

At this time, my heart beat was beating around thirty-three, where it should be a normal rate around seventy or higher. The mystery is that I had no chest pains, no dizziness, no chest pressure and no numbness. This is a silent way of a heart attack, especially in women.

By this time my family was concerned, emotional, and all I could think of was that there were a few business items that needed to be dealt with in my office, and someone had to contact my supervisors, both of them, telling them that I wouldn't be at work tomorrow, and didn't know how long I would be absent.

As the day passed, I remained in the critical care room, while arrangements were being made to transport me to Edmonton, for pacemaker surgery. At one point Doctor Karen told me that I would get the pacemaker within a few days, but didn't have a definite time. Later that evening, I was moved from the critical care room, to a monitoring room in the acute care area, to wait to be transported to the city.

In the middle of all this commotion, my sister (one of twins) and brother-in-law had been contacted by my husband, came to check on me. Everyone was standing around my bed with concern and forlorn looks on their faces. Everyone worried about my well-being. Even my two young grandchildren, standing by my bedside had serious little faces, and all I could think of was to tell them, "Grandma will be okay."

# NINE
# Closer to Heaven

Late in the evening, about midnight, the Emergency Response Team arrived with a stretcher, to prepare me for the flight to the city, making sure all wires were connected, intravenous, and electrocardiogram pads were in place. I was moved from my hospital bed onto the stretcher, not realizing I had just edged myself into a black bag with a zipper. I felt like I had just crawled into a body bag, which was not very comforting. Now covered with a blanket, I was ready to be transported to the ambulance.

As I was pushed down the hallway to the ambulance bay, my son walked beside me having a light conversation with the attendances, as he knew them personally. It gave me a great deal of comfort, however, saying good bye was difficult, especially looking at my son's solemn face. It was very hard to stay calm, as a lump rose in my throat, barely able to say, "Bye," as tears swelled up. As the doors closed on the ambulance, I suddenly realized, "Oh my god, I was in serious condition. My brain must have been in a slow mode for the past few hours, and now racing to high speed of anxiety. I would have liked to be somewhere else, at this moment."

The bumpy and uncomfortable ride to the airport, an approximate five kilometers from the hospital was quick. It was past midnight, the skies were dark with a cold west wind blowing. The cool weather resembled an October evening, not an evening in late June.

As the Emergency Response Team transported me from the ambulance to the airplane, I never realized how coordinated the Emergency Response Team needed to be when it came to maneuvering a loaded stretcher through a narrow opening of a small plane. The stretcher was moved in a way to ensure the stretcher stayed in a horizontal position, bumping, twisting and turning, and then I was stuffed through a small door. It was quite a challenge to make sure I stayed on the stretcher upright. My stretcher was placed against the wall of the plane on the right side, and the Paramedic sat on the opposite side. She checked my intravenous to ensure it was working, as the plane lifted off into the night sky, and headed south towards Edmonton. I probably should have used this time to sleep, but I was wide awake, like an old hoot owl sitting in a tree in the darkness of night. I was determined not to go to sleep, not to even relax my eyes. I just stared up at the ceiling of the plane. I guess I was unsure of my circumstances, and I couldn't stop thinking about the black bag I was laying in. I kept thinking, "Be dam if I am going to die, and be zipped up in this black bag! This gives me the creeps. I am staying awake." Although it would be a short one and half hour ride, it felt like an eternity.

Half way to the city, an electrical storm was occurring, and the plane was headed straight towards it. Lighting was continuously flashing, lighting up the inside of the cabin, then the turbulences began. At first, gentle motions, moving the plane back and forth, up and down, similar to floating in a small boat, as ocean wave's splash back and forth. Then the turbulences became stronger. At one point there was such a strong force, the plane dropped altitude quickly. My whole body lifted up off the stretcher, and if I had not been strapped in, I am sure I would have fallen off. Realizing the danger, the Paramedic put on her seat belt, as she was shifting, and sliding back and forth in her seat. This storm was serious, but the plane flew straight through the stormy clouds, like an eagle soaring steadily across the skies. As the plane approached the city's airport and landed, I silently said, "Thank you Creator, for placing me on solid ground."

I was moved into an ambulance that waited on the tarmac, and quickly transported to the Sturgeon General Hospital, in St. Albert, a community nearest to Edmonton. It was a bumpy ride, because of construction on the streets. We finally arrived at the hospital about two o'clock in the morning.

As the Emergency Response Team rushed me down the hall to the ICU/CCU area, all I could see was the white ceiling and cream colored walls rushing past me. Once in the assigned room, a number of nurses assisted the Emergency Response Team, sliding me off the plastic board onto the bed, out of that black bag, then disconnecting lines and wires, and re-connecting me to the hospital machines with efficiency. I didn't know what to expect, and by this time I was really oblivious to what was going to happen next. However, I am still thinking. "Thank god I am no longer lying inside that black bag."

Once I was settled, Doctor Azim came in to talk to me. He asked the most unusual question. "Do you remember me?" I looked at him and said, "No!" He proceeded to say that he was in the operating room, assisting with my recent surgery, which was a year ago. I thought, "How the heck would I recognize him, when all the people in that operating room were in green gowns, hats and face masks. All I could see were eye balls!"

He asked a few questions, gave the two nurses instructions, and left. I laid there in a dimly lit room, listening to the machines soft humming, swishing sounds, and wondering, "How would he remember me? Oh, he read my chart." Every ten to fifteen minutes a nurse came in to check the stats on the machines, as well as my feet. At the time, I wondered why it was so important to check my feet. I found out later, that they were checking my blood circulation and pulse. I tried to rest, but the interruptions continued, with nurses and Doctor Azim, (now I know who he is), coming in and out of my room.

Around four o'clock in the morning, Doctor Azim appeared again, and announced that he would be performing pacemaker surgery on me. He then explained what the procedure would involve. I agreed with uncertainty, as I was not really sure how pacemakers worked, and what type of procedure was about to occur while I am in my bed. So I waited for someone to prepare me for surgery. I kept thinking, "Surgery right here in my bed!"

This was a somber period for me, like I was frozen in time, alone and without sleep for the past thirty hours. Thoughts of my husband driving to the city in the middle of the night concerned me. And my children and family members waiting for a call, and especially thinking of my mom, who would be waiting for news of my condition. I kept trying to make sense of what had transpired in these past few hours.

The same two nurses, who have been hovering over me, came into my room to prepare me for surgery. All of sudden my bladder was telling me that I should go to the bathroom. I stated to the nurse standing next to my bed, "I need to go to the bathroom." Her reply was, "You are not to get out of bed, not even using a bedpan. Doctor Azim has left instructions that you are not to move. If you need to go that bad, we can insert a catheter." I quickly said, "No thanks." She reassured me that maybe it was just nerves, and I sure was hoping she was right, because I would be extremely embarrassed if I wet the bed.

The team arrived, the same two nurses who prepped me, and Doctor Azim, along with all the instruments, bandages, gauzes, and pads. All my monitors were checked, and Doctor Azim instructed me not to move, to be very still. In my calmness, and ignorance of what was going to happen, I again agreed. I couldn't believe this was actually happening to me in my bed. Holy Crap!

One nurse stood at the head of the bed on the left side, placing a pale blue sterilized twenty-four inch square sheet over my face. "Oh!" Now I couldn't see, and couldn't breathe. I am claustrophobic and panic was about to kick in. I really had to concentrate to stay calm. My most horrid fear is not being able to breathe; I needed to feel some sort of air. Recognizing my difficulty, she kindly lifted the sheet up so I could feel air; a slight breeze came in under the sheet pad. This comforted me, and helped me relax some. She continued to hold the sheet, and the nurse on my right, monitored my blood pressure, and held my hand. Doctor Azim placed a sterilized pad around my neck area, and then he quickly made an incision into a vein on my right side of my neck and threaded the pacemaker's catheter through the vein into my heart. I didn't know, but I am sure there was some kind of freezing injected into the intravenous, because I could not feel any pain. The external pacemaker was connected, the incision was bandaged, and the external pacemaker was covered, and taped to my neck. Doctor Azim instructed the nurses not to change the dressing, and not let anyone touch the area, as it could get contaminated. All the readings on the monitors improved, and my heart rate increased slightly, which was a good sign. An x-ray was ordered and in no time a mobile machine arrived in my room. I was propped up in bed; a chest x-ray was taken to ensure the lead was in the proper location of the heart. Yes! All was good. Although the lead was only marginally stable in its position, but working.

As everyone left the room the lights were dimmed, and the door was closed. I thought, "Now I can get some rest but I still felt like that old hoot owl, eyes wide open, and sleep seemed so far away." As I lay in the dimly lit room with wires taped to my chest, an intravenous stuck in one arm, and a blood pressure cuff wrapped on the other arm, squeezing up, and down, and unable to turn my neck as there was a big blob taped to the right side of my neck, which made a crinkling sound when I tried to move. My thoughts were, "How could I sleep?" Throughout the rest of the night, these same two nurses continued coming into the room every ten to fifteen minutes to check the monitors, and me. If I had thought of sleep, it was impossible with all the activity going on. The plan was that I was to go for surgery in the morning for a permanent internal pacemaker.

My husband arrived early in the morning, suitcase in hand. When he saw me, surprise was written all over his face. And his first words were, "What happened?" I must have looked like something from outer space with several different colored wires attached to me and this gadget taped to my neck. He wanted to know what took place over the past several hours, and when would I be getting a permanent pacemaker.

Since I was expected to go for surgery in the morning, there was no breakfast for me. Then I received word that I would not be getting my pacemaker that day, no trip. Later in the morning I received my breakfast, which I was grateful, as I had not eaten since lunch time the day before.

Throughout all this, I had no desire to sleep. I think I was past the period of requiring sleep, so I stayed awake all day, patiently waiting for notification when I would be transported to University of Alberta Hospital in Edmonton for my surgery.

Later that afternoon, my daughter arrived. She took one look at me, asked many questions, wanting to take care of me, and making sure I was comfortable. How wonderful, when your child wants to take care of you, it felt wonderful. Good to have family that cares.

The day went by quickly, and when the next morning arrived, I was transferred to the University of Alberta Hospital-Mazankowski Alberta Heart Institute in Edmonton for pacemaker surgery. I felt like I had just come through one battle, and going back into another one.

Since my last surgery was only a year ago, I expected similar preparation procedures, as I was wheeled into the operating room. Waiting for anesthetic, and silently lying there listening to the medical team joking with each other while preparing for the operation. I felt comfortable and relaxed. As I lay there observing, watching and listening to the instructions occurring around me, being distracted from activities that were happening near me.

And before I knew it, an intravenous was inserted into my right arm, and a local anesthetic medication Lidocaine and Marcaine (injected to numb the area where the pacemaker was to be implanted) flowed through my vein, and hurt like hell! A nurse standing close to me continued to monitor the intravenous, not saying anything, even when I commented on the sharp pain travelling up my arm. At this point I managed to refrain myself from being rude as tears swelled, and streaked my cheeks. As the pain in my arm subsided after a few minutes, I was relieved, thinking, "Thank goodness for that, or I would have been yelling at somebody."

My left arm was placed on a padded sheet, wrapped, and strapped down, leaving me with no movement. A wire frame was then placed in front of my face, covered with a sterile padded sheet. There was just enough room, a peek hole, to see across the room toward a wall, and I could feel air coming through that small space, so I could breathe without feeling claustrophobic. Knowing what was about to happen, I concentrated on my breathing, to stay calm, not to panic, and remembering to stay absolutely still. While surgery was being performed, I could hear the Doctors talking, and from time to time, I felt pressure on my chest and neck area. Then I could feel light pinching sensations from being stitched up.

Thinking back of those who I know who had pacemaker implants, never spoke of being awake while this procedure took place. No one warned me that I would be awake, and no anesthetic. However, I was not fond of anesthetic anyway.

Before I knew it, I was moved back to cardiac recovery. An x-ray and electrocardiogram were done, and then I was transported by ambulance back to the Sturgeon General Hospital in St Albert.

Even though this had been a long turmoil filled day, and before I got comfortable enough to sleep, I needed to call home to my son, and then call my elderly mother. I knew they would be waiting for my call, and, as I expected, mom was worried and waiting for news. I am sure she just wanted to hear my voice.

The result of all of this is that I have a left bundle branch block in my heart and now I have a pacemaker, due to Sarcoidosis attacking my heart. A silent killer!

I left the hospital, the next day, July 1$^{st}$, saying goodbye to my daughter, and drove home with my husband, a five hundred kilometer trip.

As we drove home, my thoughts traced the steps back to what just happened in these past few days. I mentally noted that I had an external pacemaker with a lead implanted temporarily into my heart, to stabilize, and increase my heart beat. Then within forty-eight hours later a dual chamber pacemaker was implanted. I was feeling as if I was a robot with a robotic piece of equipment inside me, controlling a part of my body. And when I was told what the cost was for this tiny device, I soon realized how valuable I might be.

"Feeling like a robot and maybe priceless!"

↔

It is said, life's journey comes in numerous ways, small ones and large ones. My journey may be the beginning of many, as I realize people may have more than one journey in their lives. "Life is so precious!"

# TEN
# Tiny Miracle Device

When reviewing the timelines of this tiny miracle - heart pacemaker, it makes me truly thankful for those who have an inventive curiosity, and forward thinking to create a functioning device, which would be effective and save many lives.

Various experimental inventions have occurred to design and build pacemakers. Historically, since the 1700's, from awkward sized contraptions which were tested externally, with continued research throughout the 1800's into the 1900's. These cumbersome external pacemakers have evolved through time, designing a smaller implantable device.

In January of 1949, John A. Hopps invented the first heart pacemaker.

September 1950, the heart pacemaker was introduced to the world.

As of January 1, 1960 the pacemaker continued to remain the same, and then in December 1970, the first nuclear powered pacemaker was discovered. And in December 1990 the device was decreased in size. Since 1990 to 2012 the pacemaker was designed smaller and easier to install.

A pacemaker is approximately two inches in diameter, a small lightweight electronic medical device that uses electrical impulses, delivered by electrodes contracting the heart muscles, to regulate the beating of the heart.

The primary purpose of a pacemaker is to maintain an adequate heart rate, either because the heart's natural pacemaker is not fast enough, or there is a block in the heart's electrical conduction system. This is done by a tiny computer to send electrical signals to the heart.

Sensors in the pacemaker also keep track of the activity level and can adjust the signals as needed. Modern pacemakers are externally programmable, and allow the Cardiologist to select the optimum pacing modes for individual patients.

Pacemakers are regulated and adapted to an individual's activities. When individuals are active, the heart beats a faster pace to meet the body's need for more blood and oxygen. However, problems with the heart's electrical system can prevent the heart from speeding up. To fix this problem, all pacemakers have a rate-responsive feature. This means they can automatically adjust the heart rate as needed. The pacemaker speeds up when the individual's active, and returns to a normal pace when the individual is resting.

Pacemakers have three optimum pacing modes of rate-responsive features; low, medium, and high. A pacemaker is adjusted to the patient's activities.

How ironic to think I made a struggling entry into this world, about the time an internal pacemaker was being invented, and ready to be used by the world. Who would have thought a pacemaker and I would meet.

↔

Most people who receive a pacemaker have a regular check-up once a year and others require every six months or more often. I am required to have a check-up every six months at the Heart Rhythm Device Clinic.

At each of my visits for a checkup, I sit in a big easy boy chair; a nurse places red and blue clamps on my ankles and wrists. This reminded me of battery cables being hooked up to a battery to jump start an engine. (Maybe because I am married to a mechanic and had helped to connect battery cables to a battery to start a vehicle.)Then an electronic wand, which looks like a hockey puck on a cord connected to a computer, is laid over the skin where the pacemaker is implanted.

Data is collected from the recorded daily data of the pacemaker. The collected data records, such things as whether the leads are functioning, number of heart beats, remaining battery life years, and if there has been any unusual activities within the heart. At the end of the testing which takes less than half hour, a printout is printed and the data from the computer is saved on an USB and stored in the hospital's care.

My very first experience with a checkup made me uneasy, and nervous, especially when I was hooked up to the computer and the nurse began to tap, tap on the computer screen.

And my very first thoughts were; I knew how computers functioned, and how they can be controlled, even when there is no one in the same room, but connected to the system elsewhere.

It reminded me of the time a remote Computer Technician was repairing, and re-setting my work computer, as I silently watched the icon move around the screen, which was quite interesting but unnerving, especially when I was not touching anything, and the Technician was located in another community.

↔

I keep telling myself repeatedly, "Yes, I trust this person, sitting in front of this computer screen, in this little room checking my pacemaker settings." Even this doesn't help me relax. "Who could relax, not me!"

↔

At one point during one of my check-ups, there were discussions of increasing the level of the pacemaker, due to my activities, as there is a low-medium-high mode adjustment on this tiny wonder machine. The nurse stated, "I must be an active person." I am thinking to myself, "I am certainly not a couch potato."

↔

Each time I go for a checkup there will be different nurses working in the Heart Rhythm Device Clinic. This particular time, the procedure of checking my pacemaker was similar. As the procedure began checking each lead (upper and lower) to ensure they were adequately working, they were turned off at separate times for approximately one heartbeat. However, this particular time once this procedure was completed I began to sweat, feeling weak, and light headed. I told the nurse, "I do not feel well and need something to drink." After my checkup was completed I left for home, still feeling unsettled. I experienced discomfort, and nauseous feeling for several days after, similar to the feeling of having a cold with bronchial problems. I continued to have palpitations, which seemed to be more noticeable, and I was not sure what was happening, so I contacted the Heart Rhythm Device Clinic, to inquire into my last test results.

My biggest question was, "What was changed? What did the nurse do?" I needed to know if there were possible changes in my pacemaker settings, and what the readings indicated. Once I explained my symptoms, and concerns my test report was reviewed, and a new appointment was scheduled for another pacemaker checkup to ensure all indicators were functioning properly. And they were.

At this appointment I found out that my lower lead in the bottom of my heart can't be turned off, as I am one hundred percent dependent upon it. Even though it was only one heartbeat, it did affect me. Thank goodness this information is recorded in my file for future pacemaker checkups. I was relieved this happened only once, but I am still apprehensive when I enter that small room for my checkup.

# ELEVEN

# Therapies and Remedies

As the years passed, and since my implanted pacemaker, I cannot have a Magnetic Resonance Imaging (MRI) test which employ powerful magnets to create images, and can damage a pacemaker.

Alternative imaging testing are required, and therefore, a series of repeated tests have been performed and continue yearly, along with additional tests to preclude and/or ensure my organs are functioning adequately.

In this chapter, I share brief overall viewpoints on different types of medical tests, which have been requisitioned by various Doctors and Specialists, (for the purpose of treating and monitoring the locations and activities of Sarcoidosis) to manage types of medicines, techniques and my medical treatment plan.

My first experience for a Pulmonary Function Test (PFT) lung test (which has become a regular twice a year routine) was in February of 2010, ordered by a Pulmonary Specialist: a soft spoken, medium built short man, who always wears plaid shirts and has a shadowed, unshaven face.

Being unfamiliar to this procedure, I was instructed to step into a clear glass cylinder shape unit with a door, called a breathing box. This reminded me of an old telephone booth before the late 1980's.

After a brief explanation what I was to do, I placed my mouth over a small round white plastic tube which is connected to a hose on the wall of the breathing box. Next a plastic clip, shaped like an office clip was clamped onto my nose, quickly cutting off my air.

Now being instructed to breathe through my mouth, which is difficult as I am not used to breathing this way, I start gasping for air. The breathing box door was closed and I felt claustrophobic, and this is the time panic kicks in. Suddenly, I had to have the door open, and I'm out of that door like a flash. I needed time to compose myself, breathe and collect my thoughts to prepare for this procedure. I had to remind myself that I can do this. Telling myself, "Deep breathe deep breathe."

Although this is a simple painless test, it took me some time to concentrate, and prepare for this procedure without becoming apprehensive. The second part of this test requires inhaling Ventaline, which made me light, headed for a short period of time, another unpleasant feeling.The finding was that my oxygen level in my lungs was lower than normal, so there for Symbicort Turbuhaelen was prescribed, a certain dosage for ten days. At this time I cannot remember the exact dosage but I began to have headaches, and feeling ill.

I contacted Doctor Ron, who then changed my prescription to a lesser dosage. After taking the prescribed inhalant for a few more weeks, it made no difference in my breathing even when walking or climbing stairs.

↔

I have always felt it is importance to keep connected to your medical team. Inform them of any medication concerns, and outcomes. Do not continue to endure taking medications that are upsetting your bodies system.

↔

As time went by, I decided to research materials on this dreadful disease, discovering Sarcoidosis triggers tiny nodules (granulomas) of inflamed tissues to develop in the body organs, and on the outer skin. These skin lesions can occur on the face, neck, arms, legs or trunk. They can range from subtle, painless rashes to deep scars.

In September 2010, I noticed lesions appearing on my face, so I immediately contacted Doctor Karen.

I had two outer skin lesions; one was on my left upper eye lid and another on the left side of the bridge area of my nose. I was fortunate that a Dermatologist from Calgary, Alberta came to Peace River Community Health Centre monthly, so an appointment was scheduled to remove these lesions.

Thanks to the Dermatologist, who took great pride in his work, the stitches were very tiny and precise, leaving no scars.

Three years after I was diagnosed with Sarcoidosis, this disease was discovered on my left lower ankle leaving a discolored reddish rash with dry skin. I was informed; individuals with more severe disease involving the internal organs often have more severe skin lesions.

My ankle was constantly dry, and itchy, even when applying various creams; to help soothe the constant itch on this area, and to prevent dryness of my skin. Nothing worked. Then I decided to experiment with Rub-A535 Antiphlogistine ointment, (an ointment usually used for temporary relief of aches and pains of muscles and joints). Wow! This ointment actually worked, and certainly made a difference. After applying Rub-A535 ointment only once, the itch dispersed immediately making the area feel drastically comfortable, only a reddish colored dry patch remains.

↔

I have had yearly, eye examination performed by an Ophthalmologist, because of a possible detached retina identified in 2004. Thankfully the results reported, were no detachment of the retina, but showing signs of tiny floaters, which required monitoring.

In 2010, I asked Doctor Dan, Ophthalmologist to check if there were any sign of Sarcoidosis in my eyes. As I had read information on Sarcoidosis, and found that this disease can be found in the eyes. And yes, Sarcoidosis was identified. Doctor

Dan prescribed Prednisone liquid eye drops of Keflex 500mg. Following the directions, each morning and evening, I faithfully squirted one drop in each eye, which blurred my vision for a second to two, then it cleared. I was monitored by repeated testing's within a three month period. Doctor Dan reported, "Good news, Sarcoidosis had stabilized, and has not spread after this treatment." However, I was left with scarring on the right eye, near the retina which didn't affect my vision. Each year I have a thorough examination to monitor any change with the retina and for any Sarcoidosis activity.

↔

In February of 2012 another test, that I endured, due to a heart concern was a Persantine Stress/Rest Technetium Mibi Spect Cardiac Scan.

A scheduled appointment was made at the Grande Prairie Hospital, a two hour trip from my home. My hopes were that I would find out why I was having a continuous heavy feeling in my chest, because, once again, my most recent X-rays indicated nothing. And being tested on a treadmill quickly resulted in findings that apparently the treadmill would not record heart problems accurately, due to the pacemaker over-rides the heart recordings. I was informed that this was going to be a long day, as these tests would take approximately seven hours. The day commenced with an electrocardiogram, and then I changed into a green hospital gown, and walked down a hall to a small room to have an intravenous inserted, along with an explanation from the Technician, what would occur, and what alternate effects may happen (re-actions are different for each person) when undergoing this procedure.

Now, off to another room where two nurses and a doctor were waiting for me. As directed, I laid on a bed covered with a white sheet, where one nurse stood, ready to initiate the liquid injection into my intravenous, in my right arm. On the left side, another nurse connected me to the electrocardiogram machine, and a blood pressure machine. At the foot of the bed, to my far right, sat the Doctor (a slim women with greying hair) in front of a monitor screen, reading my file, and ready to give directions. The Doctor said nothing to me, as if she didn't recognize my existence. She gave instructions to the nurse who was holding the injection needle to be inserted into the intravenous line, to start the infusion with Persantine to simulate stress for nine minutes, and fifty-five seconds, to achieve a heart rate of ninety-seven. The flow of fluid started to travel through my veins. Remembering my orientation, about possible reactions I needed to ask, "What should I feel or react too?" I wanted to know, and I guess I needed to be prepared for the worst case scenario, whatever that meant. No one could answer my question as to what or how I should feel, as this affects everyone differently. Now this made me feel even more nervous, and apprehensive.

The electrocardiogram machine started to roll out dotted paper, the blood pressure cuff began to pump up and then down tightly squeezing my arm. As the liquid flowed through my veins to enlarge the blood vessels in my heart, and of course, all my veins in my body, a weird sensation came over me. I felt light headed then a sudden headache and I could feel my heart palpitate. I asked the nurse on my left "Is my blood pressure going up?" She just nodded. At that moment I began to feel weird crawly sensations sweeping through my body which scared me, I was having a reaction. I felt cold and shaky.I heard the Doctor instruct the nurse on my right, "Start the counter act drug of two doses." Within a few seconds this procedure was completed, I could feel my internal body gradually relax, and calm down. I was then given another injection through the intravenous, in preparation for the next test. What I had just experienced made me feel unsteady on my feet, as if I had just come off a merry-go-round. Thankfully, these sensitivities eventually passed, and I recovered my balance back.

I was then sent down a long corridor to another waiting room to wait for a further test, and an x-ray. While sitting in the waiting room, my body still felt jittery, with a slight headache, and I felt nauseated. After a time, not sure how long, I was then called again, to a room across the hall from the waiting room, where I was instructed to lay on a narrow bed. I am thinking, "So many different rooms to go to, and up one hallway, and down another." This big white metal machine folded around me, one part came down above me, almost touching my chest. Then the machine started to rotate inch by inch around me scanning, while the Technician watched a monitor, and controlled the machine.

In a short time, I was finished with this part of these tests. My wait time was one and half hours before going back to the Nuclear Medicine Department. I was directed to go have a few sips of water. Again, after another wait time, I was called back to the Nuclear Medicine Department area for another injection through the existing intravenous which was still inserted since I first arrived at the hospital. As the injection liquid flowed through my veins, I could taste a foul bitter zest similar to sour vinegar in my month, thankfully, which lasted only a few seconds.

My wait time again was another one, and half hours, and then I was told to go have a glass of milk or chocolate milk, in order to coat my gall bladder. I said to the Technician, "I don't have a gall bladder." She responded, "Go have a drink anyway." Chocolate milk was my choice, and I sipped it slowly enjoying the flavor, but suddenly my stomach began to ache, to add to my already dull headache. There was nothing I could do about my discomforts, so I sat quietly, and waited in the lounge area until time for the next test.

Time's up, I went in for the second repeat test, and x-ray, lying under that big metal machine, with arms resembling a robot or one of those large Lego building blocks. Test completed. Technician told me, "Go have that cup of coffee, which should help with your headache." I certainly was glad these tests were completed, and I did need a cup of coffee. The intravenous was then removed leaving blood all over the arm of my gown. All I could think of was, "What a mess! And I did feel like a mess." It was a long day, moving from one room to another room, back and forth. "I felt like a Raggy Ann, all due to checking my heart's function."

It took a few days before Doctor Karen called me, informing me that there were possibilities, and options. She identified three areas of concern; firstly, I needed to consider taking blood thinners, secondly, I would be going to have an angiogram with possible angioplasty, and thirdly, a possible heart operation. The conclusions of these tests were that there was a narrowing of vessels in the middle of my heart, but it needed further exploring. I sat in my chair holding the phone receiver to my ear listening to her voice, as she continued to talk. All I could think of was, "What could this mean? Still no confirmed results, all these possibilities."

Once again, I heard that something may or may not be required; I was frustrated, because there never seemed to be enough information for me to clearly understand. And somehow there needed to be results by getting to the root cause of the problem. It always felt as if the findings were questionable until I was poked, and prodded over, and over with nothing conclusive.

Arrangements were made for me to have an angiogram. At this time I was advised not to exert myself. I continued to have low energy, however, forcing myself to continue with my normal daily routine; going to work, and volunteering within my community. Most mornings I had ample energy, no ill feelings, which was hard to explain, but then as the day continued my energy dwindled into the evening, even with minimal physical activities. Again, I had symptoms of a cold, similar to bronchial, coughing occasionally with a dry tickle in my throat, and some palpitations. At times I had a slight burning feeling in my lungs, then at times a cold feeling travelling through my chest. I would place a warming pad on my chest, which soothed these discomforts. I had no pain, only uncomfortable twinges in my lower left side rib cage, and back, similar to having pneumonia. It was like breathing in minus temperature cold winter air to the point your lungs ached with a burning frozen feeling.

↔

Everything seemed to be revolving around my heart, but the real truth was that Sarcoidosis was the demon.

↔

Before my angiogram test, I researched information on angiograms, and my findings were that Cardiac cath (catheterization) is a common nonsurgical procedure. It is done using a catheter (a long, thin flexible tube). The catheter is inserted into a blood vessel, and guided into the heart. This allows the Cardiologist to gather information about the coronary arteries, the structure, and function of the heart.

It was May 2012, when I walked into the University of Alberta Hospital for my angiogram, the same hospital where I had my pacemaker implant.

Then, I had a flashback- remembering my trip with my mom for her angiogram. I never understood the procedure of an angiogram, and its involvement or real purpose at that time, as I had taken my mom to the city for this procedure, and never thought too much about it. But now I understood why she was so anxious, and upset the night before. She knew what to expect, because this would be her third angiogram, and had experienced having stints positioned into her heart valves and having a lot of pain. Even now, I am oblivious as to what was about to happen even though I had done research on angiograms.

Arriving at 6:30 in the morning when the doors would be opened to the Diagnostic Imaging Department, to wait for someone to come and guide me to a   particular area. A porter soon arrived and announced, "Everyone scheduled for an angiogram, please follow me." I counted seven other people waiting, along with myself. We walked along the corridor in silence, then stood in line to report our names, birthdates, and then were directed to an area where beds were neatly lined up against a wall. Each bed was in a small cubical (a curtain circling the bed for privacy). There was a section one and a section two; I counted sixteen beds. My bed was number thirteen. "Lucky number," I stated. Paper work was completed, and I dressed into a green gown only, the gowns with one tie at the back. It seems that no matter what hospital you were in, green gowns were the fashion. I am thinking, "Oh, these green minty gowns!" My blood pressure was taken, intravenous inserted, and then a nurse gave an explanation on the preparation for an angiogram. My right wrist would be shaved, and of course the groin area, just in case the procedure on the wrist area was not successful, the Cardiologist would then insert the catheterization line into a vein in the groin area. As the nurse shaved my wrist, and groin area she commented on the old fashion razor she was using, something from the twenties, and that I would itch for the next couple of weeks as both sides of the groin areas would be shaved. She said, "Going to make it even, men don't understand," she really meant the Doctors. Now I was ready, prepped, and waited my turn to go into surgery, which was scheduled for nine o'clock. As nine o'clock came and went, I was bumped because of another emergency.

Throughout the day Emergency Medical Technicians and Emergency Medical Responders transported patients in.

Then at eleven o'clock, my name was called. But, no, I was bumped again. So I patiently waited unable to go anywhere, as there were wires and lines hooked to me, and I was only wearing a skimpy, green gown. By this time the fluid in my intravenous bag was empty, and I required a new bag of fluid. All around me, people were being shuffled, and wheeled in, and out, but not me. I was thinking, "I must be the lucky one, number thirteen."

Around two in the afternoon my name was called again. This time, I was finally wheeled to the operating room. All the staff were pleasant, and friendly introductions were made as to who they were and their roles. The Lab Technician moved me onto a narrow bed, covering me with a soft white warm sheet, and then off came the gown; stark naked as a jay bird under a sheet. I did not like this; call me modest. Electrocardiogram wires were hooked up, a heavier rectangular block of plastic sheet was then laid over top of my stomach area, my left arm, and right arm were both positioned into padded wire arm holders. The Lab Technician then rubbed liquid on the shaved areas (right arm and groin) at the same time. Very quick and efficient. Positioned, above me to the far left were two large monitor screens. One was for the heart functions, showing pictures of my heart valves pumping and where the catheterization line would be going to be inserted. The second monitor displayed the heart rate grafts. Doctor Neil and a nurse were located on the right side, standing near the end of my arm (at the end of my fingertips), and another nurse on my left side, asking me, "Would you like to take a valium, to relax, and calm yourself?" I responded, "No", I was now feeling tense, and a bit anxious regarding this whole procedure, and the possible outcome. I did not need any more meds to make me feel light headed and ill to my stomach. I thought I would just tough this one out. Silently I prayed, as I was scared but not sure what I was scared of.

As the procedure began, the x-ray machine was lowered over my chest area. Doctor Neil, a small framed short man who wore black round framed glasses, resembling young Harry Potter, and a young dark haired nurse stood on my right side talking to each other. Doctor Neil then informed me that I would hear talking as the procedure would be recorded.Keeping my mind off what was happening, and the sudden sharp pain from the incision, and insertion of the catheterization line into my wrist, I concentrated on the two monitors. My arm continued to hurt, worse than a cut finger, and then odd sensations travelled through my arm up to about the elbow, then again across my chest. It seemed that my inner senses were tracking this foreign object traveling through my body. Then I was warned, by the nurse standing beside me on my left side that a dye would be injected along with a medication for numbing, and I would sense a warm sensation throughout my body, and a feeling of wetness. "Great!" I thought to myself, "All I needed to think of was that I was naked, and I would wet myself." As the procedure continued, I watched the monitors, heart rate graph lines moving up and down and across. I was hoping there would be no sign of racing fibrillation, like jumping jacks within my heart. I stayed calm and motionless as I was not strapped down. I just laid there, wide awake, looking at the monitors, and listening to Doctor Neil and this young nurse talking. I thought, "I just might get a hint of what the findings are, and my right arm hurt like hell." I kept concentrating on the monitors, trying to figure out where the catheter line was located in my heart. As I watched this line move around like a wiggly worm, as I observed my heart values pumping. Quite fascinating, I must admit, and it did divert my attention off the severe pain in my arm. The exploration was completed, and Doctor Neil gave directions to the medical team, as the x-ray continued to move back and forth, monitoring the line. Suddenly it felt as if a thread was being pulled out giving me tingling sensations across my chest and through my right arm as the catheterization line was being removed. This felt like a finger nail scratching across my skin, "Ooh." Doctor Neil asked, "Can you feel that?" "Yes," I replied.

He then explained, "Good news, the valves are clear, no need for stints or repairs, however, Sarcoidosis is still causing problems, and Sarcoidosis is showing signs in another area, the septum of the heart." Doctor Neil, then said, "A complete report of the findings would be sent to Doctor Ron, and Doctor Karen within the next few days."

As this dark haired nurse wheeled my bed down the hall, back to my original spot number thirteen, she was quick to ask more questions about the disease as she had Sarcoidosis in her twenty's, which went into remission, and now had two other autoimmune system diseases – graves and dryness of the eyes. This is when, I wondered, "How many people are sufferers or survivors of Sarcoidosis. All what's, where's and who's."

Now settled back in location number thirteen, my right wrist bandaged, and wrapped tightly with a plastic blue tie strap, which looked like a zip lock tie to ensure no bleeding. My hand and arm were elevated slightly, and were continually monitored. Just after three o'clock in the afternoon, the tie on the strap was loosened. My fingers were cold, and felt swollen, but I did have circulation. Within the next hour a nurse removed the strap, and held pressure on the incision area until she was sure there would be no bleeding. Then she tightly taped a gauze over the incision.

At four o'clock, I was given a sandwich and glass of juice. By this time I was hungry, as I had not eaten since the night before. I was thinking, "A good way to diet, or maybe not." I was required to get up and walk, as I had been immobile for several hours. However, as I stood up I felt nauseated with an upset stomach, and slightly blurred vision. I steadied myself managing to walk to the bathroom and back to my bed. My arm was tender, and sore. I was given written directions not to use my arm for a week, not to lift heavy weights over ten pounds, and to monitor for bleeding, bruising and lumps. At five o'clock, I was discharged, I got dressed, and my husband drove me back to the hotel.

The next day, I returned home a five hour trip north. That evening I removed the tape, bandage, and pad. There were only indentations where the pad was, no lumps, no bruising, but it was awfully sore. But my way of thinking was, "Good signs." What was left was a small incision, and I was good with that.

↔

After surgery I had another decision to make. What medication to take, and what were the options. This involved blood thinners, a prevention of possible heart attack or stroke.

However on the flip side of this, blood thinners may cause internal bleeding. Looking at my personal history, this was somewhat minimal, so I decided not to take blood thinners at this time.

↔

Again, another test for my heart was scheduled in December of 2012; I was scheduled for a Cardiac Position Emission Tomography (PET). It is a non-invasive nuclear scan that uses Rudidium-82 (Rb-82) to determine blood flow in the heart to further review the function of my heart.

This was a voluntary participant study, to collect data on blood flow in the heart. Both Doctor Ron and Doctor Neil recommended this procedure for me.

This was all to do with Sarcoidosis causing difficulties in my heart. I was informed there were two stage protocol used to measure blood flow to different areas of the heart, using Rb-82 and a common cardiac drug Persantine (Dipyridamole).

This was a one-time test only. Prior to this scan I was instructed not to eat or drink for four hours, and not to eat or drink anything with caffeine for twelve hours prior to this scan.

Arriving at the Nuclear Medicine Department, documents were completed, and signed. At the time I thought this study collecting information would further help other patients, and better inform the medical teams.

Now preparation for the test began, as I was hooked up to the electrocardiogram wires and a small needle (intravenous catheter) inserted into my vein in my right arm. The intravenous is used to inject the tracer Persantine. I was instructed to lie on a narrow bed, and wait for the procedure to begin. Lying motionless on the bed, the bed began to move on a moveable track through a white metal tunnel. Once inside the tunnel the machine stopped, and the center part of the machine began to move around me, as the scan began.

The ninety minute test became uncomfortable, as the injected fluid flowed into my body, gave me weird sensations as the liquid travelled through my body swelling it, giving me a sudden head pain, then a head ache. I needed to concentrate, or I might become hysterical. I needed to stay calm to think of something more pleasant. I could feel my blood pressure rise, and my whole body began to react with continued restless weird feelings. I had no pain, but a cool, crawly sensation spreading inside my body. My arm, where the intravenous was inserted, felt as if it was being twisted, causing a painful sharp pinching feeling, then a cooling sensation, as the liquid flowed through my veins. I needed to concentrate desperately, or I will cry or scream. Again I'm thinking, "I need to concentrate. What can I concentrate on?" Since Christmas was only a few weeks away, I thought of decorating my house. "What will the décor be red and green or gold's or silvers? What type of cookies and squares should I make? There were a few gifts I needed to buy. What were they going to be, and what stores should I check out." Near the end of the test, I had two injections to counter-act the pain for my head and body discomforts. One nurse said, "You should go have a cup of coffee, and that would help with your headache." Then another nurse said, "No, she is scheduled for another test." I thought, "So much for this head ache, and my caffeine fix." Once the scan was completed, and the electrocardiogram wires removed, leaving reddish round circle shapes that stayed for several weeks, as my skin is sensitive. I was directed back to my cubical.

I sat on a soft, brown easy chair, quietly waiting until my next test. I used this time to reflect on what just happened. And what I just went through, knowing that I was going to have another test, similar to this one in a very short time.

I needed to come to terms with this, and my reservations to the next test. I need to calm myself finding a way to settle my inner feelings. I kept thinking, "Why should I keep going through these tests?" Although I really knew the answer, it was hope for a sign of suppression of this terrible disease. My biggest wish was for Sarcoidosis to disappear completely, with any luck.

↔

Sarcoidosis was now detected in two areas of my heart. It was first identified in the atrioventricular area of my heart in June 2010, which is why I had an implantation Medtronic Adapta Dual Chamber pacemaker, and after a test in May of 2012; Sarcoidosis was identified in the septum area of my heart.

Sarcoidosis is found in the heart perhaps five percent of people. What are the odds, that I would be one of these individuals identified with heart Sarcoidosis?

Another yearly test which I endure is called The Positron Emission Tomography (PET) CT scan, an imaging method that involves a small dosage of radioactive substance that would be given intravenously.

My third, experience with a PET CT Scan procedure came after the Cardiac Position Emission Tomography PET test, as mentioned above.

The nurse checked my intravenous, and decided not to use the same right arm, as there was a bubble showing in the intravenous line. She pulled the needle out, and inserted an intravenous into my left arm, ready for the injection. I thought to myself, "Thankfully I have good veins. Now I feel like a pin cushion, and I hate being poked."

Within about fifteen minutes the nurse returned, holding a black apparatus, which reminded me of an old black iron anvil, which blacksmiths used for iron work. She told me, this machine is used to measure the amount of radiation received as per weight of a patient. In our conversation she also explained, "Staff are tested for radiation effects every so many months, and they wear a neck and ring monitor, which is tested also." After my injection, the nurse removed the intravenous and left quickly. Now I am radio-active. No one can enter the room until my PET CT scan. The hour feels like a day, but I am comfortable, covered with a warm sheet. So I take a short nap. "I call this my quiet time."

This test took less than one half hour and once completed I was still feeling unsettled. I then got dressed, and went for my lunch. Learning from my first lunch experience after my first PET/CT Scan, and remembering how my stomach was upset, wish washy, and unsettled, lasting for several hours after eating a hamburger, muffin and coffee. I now have learnt to choose a lighter lunch, a salad and water, no caffeine drinks, and no breads or sweets. But this time was different, even when eating a lighter meal.

I left the cafeteria with my husband walking the long hallway to the parkade, where our vehicle was parked. My stomach was still upset, I felt light headed, weak, and my legs felt like rubber. I was horribly unsteady, but forced myself to continue to walk towards the parkade. Not a good idea. I needed to hold onto the rail along the hallway then nausea rushed through me, and I needed to sit down on a near-by bench. I was sweaty, hot then cold, my stomach was nauseated, my chest palpitated, and my legs were weak and shaky. I sat for a-while, deep breathing, bent over, holding my head, and hoped these feelings would pass, and I would not vomit. I'm thinking to myself, "I don't like vomiting, in fact I hate it." I had to get to the car, I'm going home, I can't go back into the hospital. I thought, "All I needed was fresh air and the sixteen hours without food, only a few swallows of water may be the problem," not thinking it may have been the two different injections I just received from these two tests.

My husband patiently waited, asking if he should call someone, but I was not going back into the hospital or maybe, I thought, "I might not be able to make it back on my own. I was not going to be put on a stretcher or wheeled in a wheel chair."

Days later, I continued to feel ill with an unsettled aching stomach, something torturing my body. A month later I still suffered with stomach aches, and at times light headedness, chest pains that radiated through my back, then under my ribs. At times my chest felt heavy with choking sensations in my throat. However, my symptom's gradually improved with time, and I could carry on with my regular routine. Medically, there were no answers why I should be feeling this way. Later I discovered any of these tests with injected foreign fluids can cause the internal body to reject the materials, and therefore cause discomforts, particularly when I had two different types of tests within a few hours apart.

Over these past years, I have become exceptionally sensitive to my emotional feelings that overcome me occasionally. I try to find ways to distract these sensitivities by concentrating on relaxing, staying calm by sitting in my favorite chair for hours, meditating, and listening to sounds of tranquility music, which have been my best healing medicine. This was my quiet time.

↔

Since Sarcoidosis disease damaged the bottom of my heart muscle called a 2-1 V heart block, resulting with a pacemaker, and now located in the septum area, continuous testing's continue to ensure stability of this disease.

↔

I have yearly echocardiogram (echo), which is an imaging test that uses harmless sound waves. It shows how well the heart muscle, and valves are working and show the size of my heart. A transducer (a hand-held device that looks like a microphone) is used to send sound waves towards the heart which creates echoes that are picked up by the transducer and returned to a computer. The computer then changes the sound waves into images that are seen on a monitor. These images help Doctor Neil, Cardiologist to evaluate the heart, and prepare a medical care plan to monitor my condition.

I have a regular, yearly echo, usually in the spring time. However, this particular time my echo appointment was scheduled in mid-November.

My husband and I had good driving weather conditions to the city, and upon arriving the streets were clear, and lawns were brown with some green patches of grass showing in areas. Sometimes weather patterns, during this time of year would vary and can be unpredictable. To our surprise the weather changed drastically overnight. I was shocked to see a thick, white blanket of snow covered the streets. Snow had fallen at least a foot during the night. The wind was blowing, snow was still falling, and traffic on the street was moving at a slow crawl. The hotel sidewalks and roadway had disappeared. So we decided to call for a taxi, but the wait time would be up to an hour. Not a good sign, especially when I could not miss my appointment or be late. We decided to drive to Hys Centre, a block off Kingsway Street, hoping not to have any difficulties on our way there. It was a slow, slippery, nerve racking ride, but we did arrive for my appointment without any delays. The heart ultra-sound test took about an hour. Then we drove slowly back to the hotel, staying overnight and travelling home the next day.

Most times these echocardiograms had no effect on me. However, this time after a few days I began to have heart palpitations which were more than usual, and I felt unsettled with odd sensations of quivering. It seemed that the ultra sound shook something up and was making me feel ill. I thought maybe it was the medications or the combination.

So I never gave it any thought, as I had experienced this before, and the Doctors couldn't detect any problems, and didn't have any answers as to why I felt this way.I had to accept these answers, and my reasoning was that it was the strong medications I was taking. And I knew it was important not to over exert myself, to stay calm and try not to have any stress.

# Life's Special Gifts

My sentiments are when an individual, who suffers silently with any type of health conditions, lifting their spirits can be by just being there, with no words, just caring can be the greatest offer to healing.

November was one of these times, I had an echocardiogram test, and for some reason I was not feeling well for a few days after the test.

To my amazement, kindness bloomed. When I returned to work, I found sitting on my desk, a beautiful red poinsettia plant. The poinsettia's red leaves presence sparkle a silent welcome back, which certainly lightened my heart.

Thank you co-workers!

↔

All my tests were to monitor, and treat the Sarcoidosis disease, as this disease has been identified in my heart, trachea, eyes, lymph nodes, and skin.

↔

Since diagnosed with Sarcoidosis, I continued to have numerous Doctor visits, and tests. From one test result to another test result, I have felt like a radiated flashing sparkle of lights shining in the night, and then looking like a checker board of bright colored spots on my organs, and then other times, I felt I looked like a Christmas tree, twinkling, dancing, bright lights, and of course, feeling like the Road Runner in the comic strip – beep beep, up and down the road.

NOW ALL I CAN SAY IS LOOK AT EVERY DAY AS A GOOD DAY!

I've seen better days,

but I've also seen worse.

I don't have everything that I want,

but I do have all I need.

I woke up with some aches and pains,

but I woke up.

My life may not be perfect,

but I am blessed.

Lessons learned in life

# TWELVE

# Power of Medicines

My journey triggered many emotions; from fears of the unknown, tearful emotions, and then denial. I have endured the stresses of numerous tests, with the hopes that this dreadful disease would suppress, and stop travelling throughout my organs like a ghost invader.

Sarcoidosis is controlled and/or suppressed first with Prednisone, then with Azathioprine Chemotherapy then Methotrexate Chemotherapy, used either by pill form or injection. Each of these medications prescribed can cause various side-effects with many of the organs, along with long term health issues.

Prednisone is a synthetic corticosteroid drug that is particularly effective as an immune suppressant drug. Because it suppresses the immune system, it leaves patients more susceptible to infections. Prednisone is sometimes called the 'wonder drug.'

Within the next few paragraphs', I will describe my experiences with Prednisone, as Prednisone affects everyone differently.

One, of many treatments began with a small dosage of five milligrams of Prednisone. Then gradually the prescription was increased to a stronger dosage of eighty milligrams, within a six month period. Not realizing what to expect was probably a good thing, because I was still in the work force, and volunteering within my community.My body gradually swelled; face, neck, forearms and stomach, where eventually my clothing became tight, and uncomfortable, and I could not wear short sleeve blouses, as my forearms were so swollen. Some days my face, mainly in the cheek area felt flushed, hot, and burning as if I had severe sunburn. This would come and go throughout the day, without warning and then other days nothing happened. My hair lost its shine, became dry, growth minimized and began to fall out a few strands at a time. And my skin became dry and itchy.

At times I would have liked to say out loud, "No, I did not have a Botox treatment." My face crease lines and wrinkles disappeared no sunken and wrinkled areas around the eyes. They were full and smooth. Who could complain about that, except my weight gain spiraled two-fold. I just kept smiling! As I knew, I had no control over what the medication was doing internally to my body; however I still hoped that the Prednisone would be effective on this silent disease.

With this constant change, I knew I had to keep myself occupied, and my mind active. So I continued to volunteer, and stayed focused on my work. As the dosage of medication increased, my body became a state of disaster: hot flashes, sweats, puffy, tightness of the skin, especially noticeable around the area of my lips when I spoke. I resembled a gopher with fat cheeks.

Six months past, now I was into a backward spiral, going from a high dosage, to a lesser dosage as the months went by. This is difficult to explain, an indescribable withdrawal.

My muscles ached, my joints became stiff, I had continuous headaches, and my whole body screamed of pain. It resembled an addiction to drugs or alcohol.

After my first treatment of Prednisone, I developed high blood pressure, low potassium, joints and muscles ached throughout my body, and my legs and arms weakened allowing me with limited strength when I tried to lift anything heavy. I was told by Doctor Ron, I would gradually decrease in weight which I truly looked forward to.

"Think positive."

My second treatment of Prednisone had an opposite effect. Since my first experience of Prednisone and its effects, I had to build up my confidence, and tell my inner self, "I can manage this medication, and its effects. This is mind over matter. Where's my courage?"

This time, a higher dosage of eighty milligrams of Prednisone was prescribed. Although, I knew what the effects were within a six month period, going from a low level to an increased high. But, I had no idea what the effects would be when starting at a higher dosage.

"Oh my god," eighty milligrams kicked my internal body like a tree branch being shaken briskly, and all the leaves vibrating swiftly back and forth with a great force. At times trembling, to the point of not knowing when it would stop. Minutes grew into hours and no one could see it visibly. It was within me, not visual but internal emotions. At times my body would shake and quiver internally, as if I was standing on a vibrating machine. Even, at times my thought process became unclear, with forgetfulness. Then I would experience wish washy feelings. I kept thinking, "I hope these meds are kicking the shit out of those Sarcoidosis nodules (granulomas) and please make them disappear.

↔

One awkward moment, while going through a down day as I called it. My inner body vibrating periodically, I was quietly sitting very still at my desk when my phone rang. I answered the call, hearing the caller say to me, "How are you doing?"

I suddenly blurted out, "Vibrating!" We laughed, as she knew my condition, and all I could imagine was my body invisibly quivering and shaking to rock and roll music.

↔

Each time I am prescribed Prednisone, which is almost yearly, either doing the uppers or downers, I become apprehensive, but I do know that this wonder drug has worked to some degree. And with Doctor Ron's encouragement, and me having determined hope there may be change.

Over these past years, there have been numerous appointments, and trips to the city, always with hope to hear positive results. And it was always in my best interest or I thought it was to stay positive, keep my spirits high with hope for good news or at least improvements. Especially after enduring different strengths of medications.

Not! Doctor Ron informed me that the Prednisone had somewhat suppressed the disease after taking it for a year, but now being off Prednisone for a year, Sarcoidosis showed an increase of activity again; however, not as high as previously. This should have made me feel somewhat better, however, when looking at the test results, highlighted bright colors (pictures on a computer monitor) dancing, and sparkling, reminded me of a checker board. "Now I looked like a dam checker board inside me."

Sarcoidosis was showing up in areas of my lymph nodes, heart (affecting heart functions), trachea, and the lower stomach area. My confidence gradually depleted when I heard this news. Why is it when it seems that, as long as I'm on Prednisone the Sarcoidosis activity minimally decreases, and then once I'm off Prednisone, Sarcoidosis begins to increase activity? My question was, "What's making my system not respond effectively?" It felt like I was dancing the old country two-step with Prednisone, two steps forward one back.

At this point of conversation, I felt disappoint, and distressed. Doctor Ron continued to discuss the next medical plan, a strategy to continue Prednisone, reaching a greater strength level, and then start chemotherapy pills. The word chemotherapy started to ring in my head, "Chemo, chemo!" This threw my whole thought process into a frenzy. All I could think of was, "Chemo was for people with cancer not Sarcoidosis." The word chemo had so many connotations. At that moment nothing was important to me; going home or any commitments to return to work the next day as planned. I walked out of Doctor Ron's office, and went shopping. This was the best therapy for me personally. I needed time to regenerate, and to clear my thoughts, as I felt drained.

↔

Even with several attempts with Prednisone which was not stabilizing Sarcoidosis, the next step was to start another type of medication.

Doctor Ron gave me material to read on two different types of chemotherapy, and suggested I look at my options. Being apprehensive to the thought of taking chemotherapy, and realizing this was the next medical step to control this dreadful disease. I carefully read all options, and then I made a decision to take Azathioprine Chemotherapy, as recommended by Doctor Ron.

I began my treatment of Azathioprine Chemotherapy by pill form, in March, 2013, along with Prednisone, Folic Acid, Vitamin D, and High Blood Pressure pills. I was now feeling like a walking drugstore with various colored and shaped pills lined up on my bathroom counter.

I continued to follow all directions including regular blood, and urine tests. However, after taking a daily dosage of Azathioprine, for about a week, again, I became nauseated, and had a burning sensation in my stomach along with an odd foul taste in my mouth after swallowing my daily dosage. I began to drink milk with each dosage, and found this was a good alternative as it soothed the burning sensation in my stomach. Gradually my taste buds decreased in identifying flavors, and as several weeks passed any consumption of cereals, yogurts, breads, especially sweet breads and now, even milk made my stomach ache continuously with nausea and at times I felt like vomiting. However, I could eat a small bit of cheese. I also stopped drinking coffee, as it caused burning of the stomach. Eventually I found soya milk worked in my favor when taking Azathioprine, but another temporary solution.

↔

By this time I started to re-evaluate what my intakes of foods were, and what nutritious foods I could eat, without having any discomforts of aching, and nausea. This became a constant challenge, experimenting with various foods.Trying different foods only helped for a limited time, and then my stomach would act up. Once again my stomach would continue to ache with occasional sharp pains, and cramps which became daily, with continued nausea, and occasional vomiting. I felt my body was falling apart; headaches, pain behind my eyeballs, as if something was pushing them forward, continued painful stomach aches, and hot, sweaty, sleepless, restless nights.

By the end of April, I felt like I had been in a ship-wreck, dumped into the sea, and swept up on the shores of some no-where land. My weight increased, bloated, and my mid stomach area swelled like a balloon. The most annoying situation was when I dressed in the morning, my clothes fit comfortably, and by mid-day, they were skin tight, as if I had gained excessive weight. My body felt like rising bread dough.

↔

This was the year, May 2013; I would be receiving employee award and retirement recognition at the School Division Award Event. This event was special to me. My day began fairly well with limited puffiness, so I selected an outfit from my wardrobe, ready for the evening event. Throughout the day my circumstances changed, I gradually began to swell with puffiness, and feeling like a dough boy. Now it's time to attend this special function and I was determine to search through my wardrobe for another outfit, thinking to myself, "I sure am glad I kept two different sizes of outfits in my wardrobe, and I am going to enjoy myself this evening no matter what."

Little did I know I was having a reaction to Azathioprine causing havoc with some of my organs? Apparently, I was being poisoned. With thanks to my weekly blood tests, and the close monitoring of these tests, Doctor Ron contacted me, informing me to stop taking Azathioprine immediately. He was ordering a battery of tests for blood, and urine, and an ultra sound for my kidneys, liver and pancreas. Alert, alert, was all my brain could register. All I could think of was that, "I am in danger, and my body was not responding well to Azathioprine Chemotherapy." My white blood cells were higher than normal. The chemotherapy was causing toxins within my body, and producing an elevation of enzymes in the liver.

The reported findings were that the liver showed fatty tissues, and the kidneys looked like there was some scar tissue, a bit of a mystery.

## Gift of Giving

I was always thankful for those who cared, and this was the time when caring people around me were the best part of my healing.

Three ladies, my co-workers kindly presented me with a yellow rose, and a bottle of white wine (my favorite). A touching moment, as they spoke, "For a private person who never complains about her condition, and courageously continues to come to work daily. Bless them."

Lifting my spirits helped me build strength, and courage to move forward, and to stay strong.

↔

Since I did not respond effectively to Azathioprine Chemotherapy, and my body rejected this medicine, Doctor Ron suggested that I should consider taking Methotrexate Chemotherapy. After having experienced Azathioprine, I was not extremely confident in trying another type of chemo, especially after I read the materials on Methotrexate Chemotherapy, and its after-effects, and particularly when I read the section about the loss of hair.

I felt unsure if I wanted to take these steps. To me it felt like a giant step to the unknown. I could just imagine looking in the mirror at myself, visualizing my bald head. I was apprehensive of losing my hair, especially my braid, which I started to grow when I was first diagnosed with Sarcoidosis.

I believe spiritually, hair is the physical expression of our thoughts, and an extension of us. In my teachings traditionally there are great spiritual values on the significance of hair.

Many may not understand, and then there are others that recognize why I chose to wear a braid. When first diagnosed with Sarcoidosis, I had a vision, to grow a portion of my hair located behind my right ear, styling into a braid. My braid(s) represent life's cycle. Braiding my hair daily comforts me as I pray for improved health, thoughts of my loved ones, and blessing those many angels; family, and friends who have gone to heaven.

After my conversation with my family, about the possibility of losing my hair, they jokingly said, "Mom we could buy you hats and make pretty bright head scarfs." I guess when your family is supporting and cheering you on, and want the best for you, how can you not continue with treatment? In reality it may not be just the thought of the loss of my hair, but how I might feel, because of my recent experience with Azathioprine Chemotherapy.

I continued to think of, "How many people do I know that have lost their hair due to taking chemo for other diseases? If others can be brave so can I even if I lose my braid."

June, 2013, I was prescribed Methotrexate Chemotherapy by pill form in a lower dosage once a week. I found that, Methotrexate medication occasionally caused an upset, nausea aching stomach, particularly after consuming foods but manageable. As I continued to tolerate Methotrexate over the next year, there were minimal results of Sarcoidosis moving into suppression. This was depressing, and caused me stress, as I was hoping for change. After a year and half of taking Methotrexate Chemotherapy in a pill form, there were further discussions with a Rheumatology Specialist, Doctor Elaine, regarding changing my prescription to increase my dosage to double, but in a liquid form by injection. Now I felt disturbed, as I was always waiting for good news, hearing the word suppressed. My first reaction was, "Okay I can handle this. What-ever it takes to get this disease into remission."

However, taking pills are one thing, and experiencing injection by a needle is another. I do not relish the thought of getting a needle, much less having to learn to inject myself. All I could think of was, "I can do this, and I am going to learn this procedure, and I will inject myself. I am determined to learn." In conversations of my situation with others, the first comments were, we could never handle giving ourselves a needle. Just the thought of it makes us nervous. And I am thinking, "Me too, but I need to do this."

It was somewhat a challenge to locate a qualified professional, in my hometown to teach me, but, thankfully I found a Pharmacist trained, and qualified for this particular type of medication injection. Going through my training, re-confirmed the realization that this was a real life experience of having to do this injection myself, and on myself. Okay, now I must learn to self-inject properly, and accept that I can do this with determination.

The Pharmacist was excellent, and especially encouraging, as she went through the instructions, preparing me for my first injection. She mentioned that if I felt that I could not inject myself, I could come to the drugstore, and have one of the Pharmacists give me my injection, as they were all trained in this area. But I am stubborn, and do have a determination about me that I can do anything, once I put my mind to it.

Now it was time to do the injection, with a needle (5/8" long) in one hand and positioning my other hand on my stomach area, pulling up the skin, where I had to inject. All I could think of, "It's going to hurt, and I don't like pain." Looking down at my stomach, my hands in position, needle pointing at my stomach, I get ready to inject myself, pushing the needle towards my skin. I stop, holding the needle in mid-air. Then I hear the Pharmacist say in a cheering way, "Go, go you can do it, go, go." I pushed the needle into my skin, released the fluid and pulled the needle out. I looked up, a bit astonished and said, "It didn't hurt."

I walked out of that drugstore, feeling pretty proud of myself. I actually gave myself an injection without feeling faint. However, the big test would be next week, when I was alone at home in my bathroom preparing to give myself an injection. This would be another test of my skills, and will power. "How strong am I going to be?" Is the question I asked myself?

Next week came, and I carefully re-read the directions which I was given by the Pharmacist. Preparing the needle was the easy part, and then it was time for the injection. I had to regain my courage, by deep breathing and telling myself, "You can do it, you can do it." As I inserted the needle into my stomach area, I could hear a faint voice chanting words, "Go, go you can do it."

Yes, I successfully completed my injection, although admittedly, I felt slightly squeeze. Oh! Now I needed to lie down. After taking a few minutes to restore my wobbly knees, I proudly say to myself, "I just accomplished a difficult task, now I am sure I can handle whatever comes my way next."

THIRTEEN
# Healing Traditional Ways

Years have passed and it was time to think outside of the traditional medication box for alternatives, and for my own peace of mind.

Since 2009 my diagnoses with Sarcoidosis, resulted with lesions on my trachea, in my eyes, my stomach area, in the lymph nodes, outer skin lesions, rashes, and a damaged heart resulting with a pacemaker.

I needed to research all avenues for alternative methods. Within, I ponder, "This is my body, and I understand my body much better than anyone else. I do know what's best at least I hope I do."

My determination was to find ways to improve my health condition, and not feel continually ill. I was driven to become my own advocate to look for alternative methods to help improve my immune system. I desperately wanted to feel better again.

Throughout my research, I continued to have open communication with my Doctors, and I was persistent to educate myself on the various medicines I had consumed. I felt this would assist me to find the right treatment. I needed to think outside prescribed prescriptions, and not have any fear that the Doctors would not understand or disagree with what I was undertaking.

↔

I visited a local health food store looking for natural herb products, to help with my energy. Through various inquiries, I managed to find a medicine made of mushrooms grown in the mountains of China, pomegranate, and ginseng mixture of natural ingredients. After taking these herbs for a week and half, I found I had more energy, and the cold feeling in my chest dissipated. I continued to take this herb regularly however; I found it was too strong, when using the full strength as per directions. So I lessened the dosage and continued taking this herb for a few months, which boosted my energy level so I was able to manage my daily routine.

↔

I caution readers, the importance to research what's in botanical herbal tincture's ingredients, as they may interact with other prescribed medications.

↔

My goal was to continue to make education and research an integral part of my treatment process, as well as part of my life wellness.

My dear friend Bernadette, gifted me a book, called, <u>Jesus Was in My Room Last Night</u>, written by Sonja C. Isaac, a Sarcoidosis survivor. One part of the book speaks of Sonja eating papaya, which she felt helped suppress her Sarcoidosis. Apparently one of the most important ingredients in papaya is the enzyme papain, shown to be effective against a number of stomach and intestine problems, such as expelling parasites to ease the symptoms of irritable bowel syndrome.

Christopher Columbus is said to have called papaya the "Fruit of the angels."

As I have been on a mission trying anything to suppress my Sarcoidosis, I introduced papaya into my diet daily, eating ½ cup of fresh or candied papaya. I found it helped with my digestive system, minimalized my nausea, and eased my aching stomach.

↔

Sonja Isaac, also spoke of Magnesium, and how it helped with her aching, stiff joints and muscles. I was at a point of trying anything as I was plagued with stiff, aching joints and muscles, for months, which disabled my movement out of bed easily, as it took minutes to become fully mobile. Sometimes tears flowed down my cheeks, from the pain. Even when I walked up or down the stairs, it was difficult. My legs hurt, with stiff sore ankles and knees. It took every effort to effectively move with some normality. After introducing Magnesium into my routine for about a month, my joints, and muscles showed signs of less stiffness, pain, soreness, and minimal cramping with my fingers (which would twist sideways without warning). I managed to walk up and downstairs, and get out of bed much easier, with less pain. I was grateful to have found information on Magnesium, as this has made my mobility more bearable.

As I continue with my research, I have introduced other vitamins and foods into my daily diet, such as Multi- Vitamins, Mega 3 Fish Oil, and I limited my caffeine intake. I also found drinking peppermint tea helped sooth my aching stomach with less nausea. I needed comfort, and finding that peppermint tea could be one of my biggest solutions for my ailments. Now when a Physician suggests another pill for my stomach, I say, "No thanks, I will drink my peppermint tea."

↔

With a lot of thought about other resolutions, I decided to schedule an appointment with a Naturopath Doctor, who may guide me through the use of Homeopathic Remedies.

What can I lose? Nothing!

I was looking for answers with hopes that perhaps Naturopath Doctor could guide me to understand the root cause of Sarcoidosis. Particularly I wanted to improve my health, and perhaps place this miserable disease into remission since prescribed prescriptions exhibited minimal responses. After having a consultation and tests with the Naturopath Doctor Tam, she then recommended that a, 'No white' eating program would be beneficial for my condition, along with a detox program, to cleanse my immune system, and minimize the mercury findings within my body. She also suggested that I find a Massage Therapist who could perform lymphatic massage.

No whites! This meant no white sugar, no white flour, no dairy products, and yeast. This was a huge step to consider, and a lifestyle change. However, it didn't take me long to consider these recommendations; admittedly, I was looking for alternatives, even while I continued with the prescribed medication.

As I said before, "What could I lose – nothing?"

Again, I was on a mission to begin a new routine, with written remedy instruction form in my procession, I began, yet another journey to follow an eating program. However, I knew that some of these foods I was required to eliminate would be difficult especially sugar. I have such a sweet tooth and love my deserts.

And I did locate a Massage Therapist for lymphatic massages. I truly felt blessed with another miracle, a holistic type of Body Talk System, a simple and effective form of alternative healthcare, which has helped immensely with my continuous aching stomach and nausea. All it took was one lymphatic massage treatment, and my aching stomach dispersed. However, I continue my treatments monthly, for the comfort of having no aching, and motions of vomiting.

Over the past year, I continued to see Doctor Tam monthly; following the program along with homeopathic remedies. My health symptoms have improved immensely with less fatigue, less pain, nausea, and my weight has stabilized. I will continue to stay intuitive, to listen to what my body's messages are, stay on track, and keep strong.

# FOURTEEN
## You Don't Look Sick!

Sarcoidosis is my culprit; an invisible disease showing no visual signs. I've been told I am a walking wounded soldier, who faces each day of the unknown as a new day, forging forward.

I refuse to allow my discomforts or any negative thoughts control me, staying brave, active, and I consider this disease a nuisance. I am not going to allow any interruptions in my life. I will pursue forward, spending each day as if no other day.

Although I appeared visibly well, from time to time, receiving compliments on how good I look, but I feel horrible on the inside. I'm like that apple or potato, looks good, smooth and not blemished on the outside, but sadly damaged on the inside.

Deep inside me I am thinking, "If you only knew. Behind this smile, the pain I feel, worries I wallow in, the fears I face, and the incompetent way I truly feel, I'm feeling like crap."

And sometimes when I say I'm okay, I need someone to look me in the eye, hug me tight and say I know you are not.

With this, I continued my normal daily routine, getting ready for the day. Even if these were my worst days, feeling sluggish, nauseated, and would rather stay in bed or not leave the house; I'm determine  to begin the day. And then there were days I had no appetite because of the painfully nauseous in my stomach, and I felt like vomiting but I knew I needed to eat to keep my strength.

↔

One of my conversations with my baby sister, I expressed to her, "I really don't know how I managed to function with my daily routine – work and home, as I was extremely unwell a couple of years ago. All the different medications I consumed caused after effects which, I dealt with. And many times these meds would cause various reactions to my body, even at times from hour to hour or minutes to minutes. I am not sure how I endured these times, but I knew I had to keep moving, and not allow this disease to conquer me. Even now I continue to endure these days of illness."

And then there was another time, I was told later, my long-time friend Bernadette explained the symptoms of Sarcoidosis to her sister Annette. Annette couldn't believe it, especially when she had a visit with me; later Annette commented to Bernadette, "I can't believe that she is actually sick. She looks really good." Bernadette commented, "She never leaves the house unless she has her make-up on, and is well dressed. Dianne still puts on her lipstick. She's a strong person and will not give up."

Although, admittedly, at times my thoughts do wonder, "What would it be like if I didn't have sarc? How would I really feel?"

So as these days pass, I continue to wear a smile on my face, but my silent battle is a continually long lonely road.

## FIFTEEN
# Spirits Calling

I am a firm believer of intuitions, premonitions, and life after death re-incarnation. Our minds are very powerful, giving us the strength to believe and heal.

As I have described my experiences of the fading out of my body, the emergency trip for a pace maker, and that black body bag. Oh that black bag! This certainly demonstrates my belief to fight the battle to live. I am convinced that I have been given the strength to effectively find concrete answers, and continue the battle to survive my disease.

Another one of these questions which keeps popping into my head is – "What does one believe in? How to interpret messages?"

↔

A few weeks after I had my pacemaker surgery, I was having coffee at a local coffee shop, when I was greeted by an old acquaintance. She expressed her pleasure at seeing me. She had heard that I had passed away and hadn't heard any more information. My first initial reaction was emotional shock, almost traumatizing me to hear this. I could not speak for a moment, as she hugged me. All I could think of was that, "I was glad to be standing there, smiling, alive and breathing."

Then, I had a frustrating telephone conversation with Doctor Ron, my Pulmonary Specialist, about not having any concrete results, as Sarcoidosis was not showing any signs of going into remission. Since first diagnosed in 2009, I have had minimal results, after numerous times going on and off Prednisone. He expressed, in a stern manner, "If it were not for the prescribed medication, Prednisone, you would not be here." To me this was a message of not being alive.

I could not believe what I had just heard. I sat listening in silence not knowing what to say. After I hung up the phone, still in misbelief what I had just heard, I needed to absorb these words. And being shaken by this, I sat in my chair, and wept, letting my tears flow, cleansing the sorrow I felt. It seemed that everything's going wrong. My thoughts kept repeating, "I am determined that no-where in my future I was going to give in. I am a fighter, and will fight my way through this disease no matter what."

Months later, again, on a tele health conference call, with Doctor Ron, who voiced that he was convinced if it wasn't for the Prednisone, I would not be here. Again, this was disbelief to hear out loud, as I choked back a lump in my throat. I was living with a mystery.

This is a man, who has encouraged me, helped me understand what was happening inside my body, and what medical steps needed to be taken. He called me, "SPECIAL." Doctor Ron knew my condition was at a higher risk level, and knew what I have endured through several medications, and tests which would cause anyone to give up.

(All being experimental as there is no cure for this disease), All this, because my life was threatened. I asked many questions, and wanted direct answers when it came to my invested interest with my health, and what other medications could be used to get this disease into remission quicker. "I do not give up." These medications have been difficult to tolerate, with many different effects. So occasionally Doctor Ron would call me to see how I was managing with the meds, giving me encouragement to have faith in the prescribed medications. Truthfully, there were no other medications to treat Sarcoidosis, he knew it and so did I.

My feelings were that sometimes life is to be heard, at other times it is to be seen, and almost always it is to be felt. Our inner spirit will guide us, become more aware, and move toward understanding oneself.

In conclusion, my theory is to not become an invalid, and let this disease control me. I will continue to carry on the best I can, and do whatever comes my way: take a holiday, visit family and friends far and near, go camping, fishing, spend time with my children and grandchildren, and spend time at my favorite coffee shop, visiting, and drinking decaffeinated coffee or peppermint tea.

All I can say is to keep focused, to have a positive attitude, and stay motivated, and don't let Sarcoidosis disease rule your life.

EVERY PERSON

IS

BORN WITH GIFTS

LIFE

IS

THE MOST PRECIOUS OF THEM

# SIXTEEN
## Living with Sarc

I am an optimist, and believe the disease will be suppressed or move into remission, longer than only a few months.

As I continue to suffer from this chronic Sarcoidosis, an autoimmune disease characterized by tremendous amounts of inflammation, I know that many of the medicines that treat this illness are almost worse than the illness and there is no cure.

The days can be long, some days are short, but always a constant reminder of the uncomfortable sensations of nausea, heaviness, itching, aches, pains, and stiffness. At times I feel consumed, swallowed up, and become annoyed with the amount of mediations prescribed, multiple tests, injections, and blood drawn. There are times when I want to yell, scream and stomp my feet at this unforgiveable demon.

The most frustrating part of this disease is that, as I am sure for other sufferers, is the unknown, the shadow of mystery.

I feel like there's a battle raging on inside of me, and I have no control.

I think of this disease as tiny particles of inflammation slowly growing, spreading across, and inside my organs, like a pooling of glue, sticking to the nodes, damaging, and restricting the organs to function effectively.

I think of all the treatments I have endured, and with the many types of chemicals injected into my veins, flowing through my blood stream, I plead, "There must be a solution."

Again I have more questions – "Why? When?"

It's a constant reminder to keep focus, keep mentally, spiritually, emotionally, and physically active, NEVER LOSE SIGHT OF THE PURPOSE.

Living with Sarcoidosis, has given me strength to persevere, to continue to research avenues to survive this disease, read testimonials from other sarc sufferers, to encourage other sarc sufferers to continue their personal research, and have interactions with their medical professionals. Also, encourage sarc sufferers to take the Flu and Pneumonia Vaccines, and with good faith this disease will be suppressed, or go into remission for an extremely long time.

↔

Remember, when you're thankful for what you have, support from your family and friends; your rocks, you are always rewarded with more.

To the reader, Sarcoidosis can affect people in many different ways, internally, externally, emotionally, physical and even spiritually.

Pray for a cure.

# SEVENTEEN
# My Many Rocks

I have learnt over time, not to take anything for granted, as life can change in a flash.

I do realize I have been blessed with many rocks in my life; little rocks, big rock, far and near rocks.

Throughout my whole life, I'm truly grateful for my family. And I know I have other rocks surrounding me; my friends and co-workers giving me re-assurance, and encouragement who would be there for me if I asked them. These are my rocks!

My days change health wise with ups and downs of various symptoms of illness, caused from the effects of the numerous medications I take, and Sarcoidosis. I knew this was affecting my family, especially my husband as he continuously asks how I'm feeling, and at times hovering over me with concern. I knew he's feeling stressed, as there really was nothing he could do to ease my discomforts. I often never mentioned how I actually felt, as this would only add further stress.

I learnt to go along with the flow of any daily activity, and suffer in silence. Sometimes this was good; as it kept my mind occupied. Mindfully, I wanted to stay strong enduring each day, not to complain out loud, keep active, and my mind off what really was happening to my internal body. I needed to move on. Being diagnosed with a debilitated disease, and at times the medications became grueling to endure; all I wanted was to have my family close to me. I needed to hug, touch, and smell each of my children, giving me a feeling of re-assured comfort with their closeness. For whatever reason or maybe this is a mother's intuition, the need to be close, even by standing or sitting near them gave me great comfort.

My most tender moments are spent with my grandchildren; cuddling, hugging, grandma's little helpers in the kitchen baking donuts, and watching them enjoy their favorite sport – dance and hockey. Their smiling faces and their stories of the day were like a ray of sunshine coming through the windows. Just being in the same room with me, would make all my pain, discomforts and worries disappear. Grandchildren are like a great spirit, being the unknown greatness on this earth. I call them, "My heavenly little rocks."

All in all, discussing life's decisions with my husband, we have come to terms that we need to do what we are inspired to do. As there is an old saying, "Can be here today and gone tomorrow." There is no need to worry about what if's, remembering we are the keepers of our own destiny. Take risks and enjoy life to the fullest.

All my Rocks in my life make me smile.

# EIGHTEEN

# Moving Forward – Turning the Page

My alterative quest is to move forward turning the pages to continue to stay strong, have faith and hope.

As this is my on-going journey, living with Sarcoidosis, it's been difficult to explain, and for others to understand. With a series of tests, at various times, and some becoming regulars, blood tests (from weekly to monthly), surgeries ( more than one), different types, and changing of medications; what works, and what doesn't work, and how each medication can, and has upset my body's natural functioning system.

Tolerating these powerful medications has been my worst nightmare, because of the unknown effects. Especially feeling a constant illness, fatigue, and at times feeling like a zombie, going through the motions of the day.

Essentially, Sarcoidosis disease will never disappear; it may go into remission, but stays in the body forever. All that I have endured over these past years, has given me definite strength, hope and encouragement to move forward, as there is a purpose for everything.

We are given the empowerment over our own thinking, balancing our mental, physical, emotional and spiritual health aspects of our life.

I have made a decision not to take this disease too serious. I will live my life as if there is no disease, not to allow the entry of these darkest moments. I've learnt to embrace the chaos of a life threatening disease, by continuing to spend quality time with my family and friends, staying active and to think positive. "I am not a sick person!" Even though, I know Sarcoidosis is my darkest shadow which will follow me to my death.

I believe connecting to life's learning's can inspire those struggling with Sarcoidosis, to keep an open heart and mind to live a full productive life.

My message is to inspire those of you who are struggling with Sarcoidosis or any other type of disease, keep strong, you are not alone. No matter what type of disease you are suffering, it is especially important for you to have a positive outlook while maneuvering through today's complicated medical environment, and focus on self-healing. One cannot conquer everything at one time, take steps, look deep into your inner-self, search your spirit, calm yourself, relax, and find peace. Life will progress forward optimistically.

I truly hope that you come away from this book aware of the innovative responses to manage Sarcoidosis or any other disease, which  may help you manage your own condition, reduce symptoms, and perhaps most importantly give you hope.

Life moves forward as I move into my seventh year battle. I continue treatment of Prednisone, which I now call,

"My Buddy," and yet another medication, Mycophenolate in effort to force Sarcoidosis into remission. I have been informed by my Specialists, that if Mycophenolate becomes ineffective, there are two more types of medications to consider. This is a sign; I am reaching the end of medication solutions. May the holistic traditional medicine make a difference?

'I will be that warrior standing strong.'

I do not know how my story will end, but there is nowhere it will ever read, "I gave up."

'Hope, Believe, Faith and Love. '

Today

I give thanks

to everyone

who are

part of

my life's journey

APRIL

IS

SARCOIDOSIS AWARENESS

MONTH

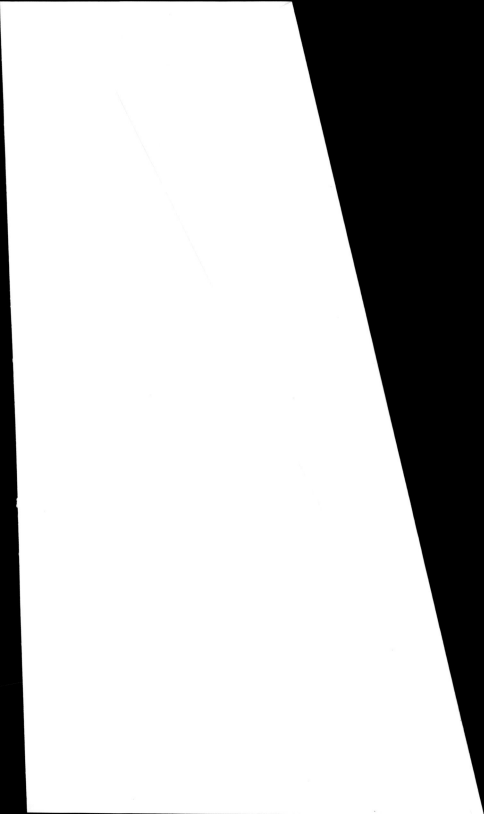

Made in the USA
Middletown, DE
12 March 2018